Being an Aroma of Christ is a book t
wiv s for whom it is written but by e
wife struggling with role identificati
ments of life in Eastern Europe, Karen acknowledges her own vulnerability
and failures but discovers that significance and victory lie in walking with
Christ and in becoming a reflection of His presence. This is the essence of
one's calling as a Christian.

Jerry A. Rankin, President
International Mission Board, Southern Baptist Convention

Clear, transparent, and insightful! Without pretense Karen Pearce commu-
nicates the challenges, costs, growth, and fulfillment that accompany cross-
cultural, incarnational service. Karen knows and understands the identity
and parenting issues of cross-cultural workers—especially the moms.
Every new or candidate missionary, missionary sender, and missionary supporter should read this book, as well as those who will serve overseas via
business, government, or non-profit/NGO's.

Rodney Hammer, Regional Leader
Central and Eastern Europe, International Mission Board, SBC

Being an Aroma of Christ is a personal testimony interwoven with deep
spiritual insights—a recipe for godly living in any culture. Page after page
carries helpful, practical preparation for a missionary wife (and for her husband's understanding) before she goes to the field, as well as for the church
people back home who will be her caregivers.

Neal and Yvonne Pirolo
Founder and Director, Emmaus Road International

This is a must-read for every missionary! I was encouraged, touched, and
inspired by Karen's honesty and transparency. She definitely is the real
deal. No doubt, this book will deepen your walk with Christ and will
expand your sweet-smelling influence for Him. Excellent material.

Steve Hunter, Associate Professor of Psychology and Counseling, Dean of Students
Criswell College, Dallas, TX

Anyone considering missions will benefit from this book's honest account
of life experiences and personal spiritual discoveries while he or she lives
on the edge for Jesus, lover of the world.

Kim P. Davis
Author, *My Life, His Mission*; Compiling Editor, *Voices of the Faithful*

At last—a book for missionaries that is painfully and humorously honest, a book that describes the difficulties of missionary life with candor and compassion, a book that challenges missionaries to glorify Christ by explaining biblical principles rather than spouting pious platitudes. Karen and her husband offered our family invaluable counsel as we served God alongside them in Romania. Now all missionaries can learn from their wisdom.

Dr. Charles Quarles, Vice President for Integration of Faith and Learning
Louisiana Baptist College

This book is an honest portrayal of the struggles and joys of life on the mission field. Karen tackles issues squarely as she focuses on God and His rule in our lives. I wish I'd had this when I moved to the mission field!

Jill De Haan, The Evangelistic Alliance Mission
MK Educator

Honest, insightful, practical and a *great encouragement* are the best words to describe this excellent resource, which is designed to help others deal with the struggles and challenges of serving in overseas ministry.

Laurie Barnes, Librarian
Institute for Christian Resources, Prague, Czech Republic

Karen Pearce has managed to hit the nail on the head—on purpose, our task is to *be* transformed into His likeness, NOT *doing* great things for the Lord. Karen then applies this concept to all areas of our lives. A "must-read" for all who live cross-culturally.

Leslie P. Johnson, Principal, Christian International School of Prague
Mission: International Institute for Christian Studies, Overland Park, KS

Being an Aroma of Christ not only is an engaging book and an interesting read of Karen's own trials and triumphs in the mission field, but it also offers solid advice and soul-searching questions for others. This book will help you find your way in your own mission work as well as bring you closer to Him.

Barbara Thomas, Teacher
Woodstock International Christian School, Mussoorie, India

This book is a huge value to women who anticipate moving to the mission field and even to those who are on the field. Her vivid descriptions brought back all the memories that I felt during the first years of our service. She writes with candor and honesty and always points to our need to depend on Christ. It speaks truth to any planning move to foreign soil as a missionary.

Tawnya McSheffrey
Serving with Josiah Venture to reach the Youth of Eastern Europe

BEING AN
AROMA
of
CHRIST

How to Survive and Thrive
while Ministering Cross-Culturally

KAREN PEARCE

Printed in the United States of America
by Lightning Source, Inc.
Cover design by Dennis Davidson
Except where otherwise indicated, Scripture taken
from the NEW AMERICAN STANDARD BIBLE, Copyright
1960, 1962, 1963, 1968, 1971, 1972, 1973, 1975, 1977, by the
Lockman Foundation. Used by permission.

Library of Congress Control Number: 2006932003
ISBN 0-929292-31-6

Hannibal Books
P.O. Box 461592
Garland, Texas 75046
1-800-747-0738
www.hannibalbooks.com

Dedicated to

my husband, Preston—
partner, Paraclete, lover, and best friend.
You complete me—and you smell great!

Acknowledgements

No work is the product of a single person. Through their involvement in my life, many have contributed to this book. A special thank-you goes to—

• Diana Paxton—my precious Romanian friend, who lived with me through the toughest times, challenged me, prayed for me, made me laugh, and critiqued this book as I wrote it.

• Mary Goodlin—my friend and mentor, who took me under her wing and loved me when I was a young pastor's wife. Her wisdom and support have blessed my life.

• Sherry Elledge—one of my prayer partners, who has been a constant source of encouragement and has prayed for me consistently throughout the last several years.

• Esther Waldrop—one of my missionary colleagues in Prague, who believed that this book needed to be published. Without her encouragement I may never have pursued it.

• Annette Helms—a missionary colleague in Romania, who put me in contact with Hannibal Books and who, on the way, tutored me.

• All the original recipients of the Aroma newsletter— Melissa H., Cheryl, Jeannie, Joy Lynn, Kim, Mary, Melissa L., Merribeth, and Sherry. The newsletter was the first draft of the book, as I worked through difficulties and shared insights with you. Thank you, ladies, for reading, laughing, praying, encouraging, and loving me.

• Kay Moore and the staff members at Hannibal Books for their patience and diligent work in making this book a reality. Thank you for opening this door for me and helping me walk through it.

• My mom—for her sacrifices, love, encouragement, and prayers. Many years ago she released me to God and to His call on my life, but doing so wasn't easy. I am so grateful for her sacrifice, obedience, and support.

• My sister, Janet—my best girlfriend and my favorite person with whom to laugh. She was a great source of strength as I worked through God's calling. I am so grateful for her listening ear, her compassionate heart, and mostly her own desire to follow God no matter what the cost.

• My children—David, Lauren, Jessica, and Andrew—for loving me despite my faults and bringing me greater joy than I ever thought possible.

• My wonderful husband, Preston—for demonstrating to me a love so unconditional and complete that through it I grew to understand God's love for me.

• And lastly, my daddy—who went to be with the Lord two years ago. I miss him so much but rejoice that he is in the presence of Christ and therefore understands with complete clarity the pure aroma of Christ.

Contents

Foreword

The secret is out! Missionaries are real, live people. They are pilgrims on a journey; they arrive at a long-awaited destination not as finished products of perfection but as fragile works in process. The one who has answered the call to cross-cultural ministry is not supernaturally immune to anger, fear, loneliness, discouragement, or pride. Overseas ministry has a unique way of exposing issues which a person may have considered conquered or buried.

In this book Karen Pearce transparently reveals the everyday challenges of missionary life. Written from the perspective of a wife and mother, her valuable insights equally are applicable to anyone involved in ministry. Candid, honest, and credible, Karen's reflections of her early years in Romania are not an expose or therapeutic ventilation of confessed failures. Instead they are components of a woman's authentic journey of faith. Stress factors include learning to relinquish her own professional identity and subsequently relating to her husband's ministry in a biblical support role. Parenting in a foreign culture, relating to churches and national believers who do things much differently, and becoming spiritually depleted when worship opportunities are in an unfamiliar language all are struggles not unique to Karen's pilgrimage. Through experiences she deems as desperate failures, Karen begins to see herself as God sees her—a transformation in process.

How I would have benefited from Karen's personal insights 35 years ago when I went to the mission field! Her life story, coupled with insightful biblical applications, would have prepared me better. Karen's response to a totally new culture and language, temporary loss of personal identity, and guilt over leaving family brought back painful memories of my adjustments as a new missionary in Indonesia. Knowing that someone had faced similar challenges and not only had survived but thrived would have been a welcomed light at the end of the tunnel.

Personal expectations can be both idealistic and unrealistic. Through reading her sometimes painful pilgrimage and cross-cultural learning experiences, you will appreciate and embrace Karen's discovery that the ultimate goal is to know Jesus. More of Him always is the answer. This knowledge of Christ—this absorption of His aroma—occurs through time spent on our knees and in the Word of God. When the heart's desperate cry becomes "Jesus", authentic joy is found in Him alone. Any other substitute is counterfeit. Get ready to be enlightened, encouraged, challenged, and changed as you contemplate the cost and blessings of being the aroma of Christ.

Bobbye Rankin, First Lady
International Mission Board, Southern Baptist Convention

A Letter to Readers

As I have sat before my computer while writing this manuscript, I constantly have been reminded of how unqualified I am to undertake this writing task. After I finished my work, I shared it with a friend. Several weeks later we were discussing our roles and ministries we would have in the upcoming year. I was feeling a little anxious. She said, "I like what you said in your book about . . .." I was left thinking, *Oh, yeah. I did say that. Then why am I anxious?* In other words, I'm still learning about my subject matter! By no means have I arrived.

Recently I sensed God saying that the time was here to share with others all He had been teaching me. The past few years have been a workshop of learning. I now see the possibility that God did not allow all of those teaching times for my benefit only but also for the benefit of others who find themselves in my shoes. I am thrilled that God might want to do something beyond me with the experiences that I have had, many of which left me feeling as though I had sorely disappointed God (though I knew that that was not really possible) and that I was useless to Him. As you will see, this is not so much a chronicle of my successes as it is a chronicle of my failures and what God, through them, has taught and is teaching me.

I have tried to be transparent with you in hopes that you might see yourself in me. If, when you read this book, you think I'm a crazy woman and hope that no resemblance exists between us, then pack the book away and get it out again after you've been on the mission field for about a year. Then you will have a new understanding of sanity and will be able to relate to me on a whole different level. I don't say this to scare you. Overseas missionary work is the greatest privilege allowed to anyone. You will have the opportunity to be on the cutting edge of what God is doing in this world and to be on the front lines against Satan and what he is trying to do as well. You will see the reality of how important abiding in Christ is and the devastation that is possible if you don't. You will see the most awesome spiritual victories and will struggle through some painful defeats. You can't hope to embark on such a journey without some struggles and some failures. What you hold in your hands is my attempt to prepare you for some of these—or if you're going through them, to understand them better—and to know, once they occur, that you are not alone in your struggles. Neither do you celebrate your victories alone. A great crowd of witnesses is around you; those witnesses know the struggles and joys ahead and the lessons to be learned. But most importantly they know, as I pray you will, too, that God surely will walk with you each step of the way; will glorify Himself through you—sometimes in spite of yourself, and will use each success and failure along the way to make you more like Jesus. Enjoy!

On the journey,
Karen

Introduction

Smelling Sweet

When I was a teen-ager, I had a part-time job at the big variety store in town. Every Friday afternoon a particular group of people arrived at the store to cash their paychecks. We always knew when these guys were in the store, because they worked at the onion-packing plant. From a mile away you could smell them. They spent their entire day holding, touching, and packing onions; that smell rubbed off on them, their clothes, their hair—even their paychecks. They carried with them the aroma of onions, because for such a long period of time they had been closely involved with onions. They didn't enter the store and try to smell like an onion. They didn't take classes on what onions smell like. Their aroma was a natural outgrowth of where they spent their lives—day in and day out.

This is the picture I envisioned when God began teaching me about being an aroma of Christ. Second Corinthians 2:14-15 (NIV) says, *But thanks be to God, who always leads us in triumphal procession in Christ and through us spreads everywhere the fragrance of the knowledge of him. For we are to God the aroma of Christ among those who are being saved and those who are perishing.*

Are you an aroma of Christ? When you become a Christian—or even a missionary, being an aroma of Christ doesn't automatically happen. Even as you approach them do people sense something about you, as we could those folks in the store? We didn't have to wonder where they had been. What about you? Can people you know tell that you've been sitting at the Master's feet? You can't fake it. Every time, you'll be found out. That's the unique thing about an aroma. Either you have it or you don't. You only acquire it one way—by absorbing it from the Source. In 2 Corinthians 2:14-15 note that the knowledge of Him—and not us—is what is fragrant. Only when we have this knowledge of Him—not about Him, but deeply, intimately *of* Him—hidden deep in our hearts is when we become aromatic.

Many people think that a ministry is the same thing as an aroma—an expression or fruit of your devotion to Him. But a ministry can be faked. Lots of people out there have great ministries. They have a lot to write home about—lots of numbers, lots of disciples, lots to show for their effort, lots of church members. They are considered successes—great Christians, models for others. But how many of those end up in disgrace and are compromised morally or discouraged in the work? They have attempted to do something FOR God instead of learning to be IN Him. A huge difference exists in the two. They may have a lot of tangible results to show for their work, but He is not pleased. And it isn't about us. It's about Him.

In the Second Corinthians verse, seeing to whom the aroma is drifting is interesting. Not to the world, missionary, because it isn't about those people; not to the church, preacher, because it isn't about those folks, either; but to God Himself. It's all about Him. It is to Him that we smell sweet. He is the recipient. And it is He—not us—*who spreads everywhere the fragrance.* It is not our work; it is His work through us. He *leads us in triumphal procession in Christ.* It is His victory—His success. Our most important task is absorbing Him and being transformed into His likeness, not doing great things for Him. He can deal with the doing, but we are to love Him so much that we sit before Him, worship Him, adore Him, learn His ways, memorize His words, and dwell on His promises. That is our task.

Now I know what you are saying. That sounds too easy, doesn't it? But you know what? Doing this is the most difficult thing in the world. Even though I firmly believe in what God has shown me through these verses, my biggest struggle still is in not "doing" enough for the Lord. Because people are results-driven, we want to succeed; we want a way to measure our successes. Being an aroma is not that kind of thing, so we feel as though we aren't doing enough.

When I first began to understand this principle, I was in America on Stateside assignment. I had prayed that God would give me a particular message to share with the women to whom I would speak and minister. God answered that prayer through introducing me to 2 Corinthians 2:14-15. As I began to understand this Scripture, I realized that this verse was the culmination of all that He had taught me during my first term on the field. I arrived in the U.S. eager to share that God did indeed have a purpose in all my struggles (and victories) during the previous three years. This understanding transformed me. I couldn't wait to see how it would transform others. As I shared these truths with other Christian women, my heart was at peace; thus I thought that surely I had learned the principles of which I spoke. I finally was resting in Him. I could see His hand at work in me and through me; I wasn't even trying. I was abiding in Him, but I wasn't out trying to do something for God. I was resting while God did all the work. I was so excited that I finally got it!

But when I returned to the mission field, I began to struggle again with the doing.

Maybe it's the word *missionary* or *Christian worker*. The very terms themselves imply doing.

Maybe it's the newsletters/prayer letters that we send home. I certainly want something significant to report. How significant is "I rested this month", or even worse, "I smelled good"?

Maybe it's because of others' expectations—"Wow! A real, live missionary! I admire you so much!"

Maybe it's because of my own expectations. Often my life as a missionary seems too normal. If I'm not leading numerous people to the Lord every week, I feel a pang of guilt for not living up to my image of being a missionary. As a mom, my focus in ministry often is our neighborhood, select women that I can disciple, and my own family. I see God at work in these places, but we haven't seen any dramatic conversions or weekly baptismal services. And often those with whom I have spent the most time seem to be struggling in their walk with God. I tend to wonder if this is because of me—if somehow I am not bold enough or sensitive enough or spiritual enough to have helped them grow strong in the Lord. Maybe I have failed, after all.

So even though being an aroma sounds as though it is a wonderful idea, I keep wanting a "how-to" plan—something practical that I can wrap my head around. It is so nebulous that I can't gauge my success at it. You can't judge your effectiveness at being an aroma as you can with more tangible things, so feeling successful often is difficult. Your measuring stick can't be the outcome of a situation or the reaction of another person to you, because you can't control those things and you don't necessarily know what God's purpose is in any given situation. Your standard has to be the Word of God. Unfortunately whenever we measure ourselves against the Word of God, we find ourselves lacking (thank God for grace!), so again, we don't feel successful.

Fortunately Scripture gives us some good guidelines for gauging success, or at least how not to. Look at Peter. Here is a guy who fails in a big way. He was under the teaching of the Son of God Himself and was so sure of His loyalty that he even bragged about it to Jesus. And yet when he failed, Jesus didn't condemn him; He restored him. Jesus wasn't keeping score or giving trophies for the greatest disciple. He allowed the failure to teach Peter. After his restoration Peter was expected to continue ministering to others. He wasn't disqualified for failing. In fact he probably learned a very valuable lesson about abiding in

Christ's strength and in not relying on his own. *So perfection in behavior can't be our measuring stick.*

What about Jesus Himself in the same situation? For three years He was the teacher, yet one of His disciples failed the test. Did His ministry to Peter fall short? Is that what caused Peter to be weak in his faith? Does Jesus indicate that He judged Himself or His success by Peter's failure? No. In fact, in John 17:4 (NIV) Jesus says to God the Father, *"I have brought you glory on earth by completing the work you gave me to do."* Jesus had completed His mission; He knew that Peter would fail. *So the behavior of someone we are discipling can't be our measuring stick.*

Paul is another good example. We all know that he was a great Bible teacher. Yet the very reason we have the great teachings from him is that he was writing to the churches that he had established. He wrote them because they were having problems—they were struggling, failing, sinning. But we don't see Paul measuring his own success by their failure. In fact he encourages us to be like him (Phil. 3:17) and dies knowing that he has completed his service to God in a pleasing way (Rom. 15:17-19; 2 Tim. 4:7-8), *so the growth or maturity of the church can't be our measuring stick.*

What about John the Baptist? Jesus said that no one was greater among men, yet he lived like a beast and had no social life. *A comfortable life or material blessings can't be the measuring stick.*

What about the prophets? God's people—who should have received them—rejected them. *So a good reputation among the brethren can't even be our measuring stick.*

The Word of God is clear, but don't we try to measure our success by these very things?

I love what Paul says in 1 Corinthians 4:3-4 (NIV), *"I care very little if I am judged by you or by any human court; indeed,*

I do not even judge myself. My conscience is clear, but that does not make me innocent. It is the Lord who judges me." Paul understood that we must stay away from gauging our success by human standards. God Himself judges us; He doesn't measure success as we do. In the end He wants to see a heart that has been conformed and shaped to the image of Christ. This is God's purpose for me and for you. We are not to abide in Christ so that we get results in our work. We are to abide in Christ so that we begin to be transformed into His image—we begin to look like Him, sound like Him and yes, "smell" like Him. This is enough. This is the ultimate. If we truly become mirrors of Christ—of His love, His compassion, His integrity, His perception—we will see God bring a world to Himself. We will have the honor of being part of His work. Yes, we will be imperfect; we will make mistakes; we will fail; we may go through times in which we don't feel very close to God. But we can rest assured that if we continue to sit at His feet, He is able to bring glory to His name through us wherever we are—whether in our marriage, with our kids, among non-believers, in the church, even sitting in traffic. He can receive glory if we are to Him an aroma of Christ—filled with the knowledge of Him.

This is really important to understand before you embark on the task of being a missionary. Probably in this field more than in any other, the expectations placed on you by yourself and others are incredibly high; the measure of success often is incredibly vague. This especially is true of women, because we are mothers and keepers at home. In many ways, no matter where we live our task doesn't change. During the times when the culture shock is especially difficult, you easily can wonder why God has you there, when you find nothing tangible to show for your personal work. Seemingly the things to which you can point to as your accomplishments could have been done, and maybe done better, in America. So why did He want you in a strange place? We long for something to make us feel significant—something to make us feel as though we've earned the admiration of the folks back home and the money they put in the missions offering each week.

For some the accomplishment of their husbands is enough. But for many of us that call to missions was very personal; we want to see ourselves being used. These desires, which begin as honest and true yearnings to obey God, often become the catalyst for doing things in our own strength and filling our time with tasks that God has not given us to do. If we will but wait on Him and learn of Him, He will bring to us the things we are to do. We don't have to find a ministry to justify our presence. God has brought you to that place for a reason. If you wait on Him, He will show you what that reason is. Your impact will be far greater if you are fragrant with the knowledge of Him in every situation than it will if you frantically look for a way to be a blessing to these Christians you're there to serve and the lost you're there to see saved.

Make this the foundation for your entire ministry, whether overseas or in America. It's not about us. It's about Him.

Following Christ is a great adventure—full of joy and sorrow, pain and comfort. As a missionary, you will see yourself at your absolute worst and you will see God at His greatest. And then sometimes, God will give you a glimpse of what He is accomplishing in you and through you. The joy is indescribable. Sometimes being aromatic seems almost impossible because you merely are trying to survive. At other times the sheer joy of being a part of what God is doing will leave you speechless. But remaining in Him is the key to success. He will protect and guide you. He will hem you in behind and before.

Chapter 1

Great Expectations

When God called me to be a missionary, I was 22 years old. Though I was surprised at God's plans for me, the adventure seemed very appealing. I could see myself blazing a trail to an unknown tribe in some remote jungle. I'd live in a hut, cook over an open fire, have evening pow-wows with the village women (who, of course, were new converts and would love me immensely), and watch my children running free with the elephants in the wide, open spaces. My kids would be perfectly adjusted to this savage life and would lead the village children to the Lord.

Can you guess that my expectations and reality were a little different? Imagine my surprise when I got off the plane in Bucharest, Romania, a city with 2.4 million people, and went to live in an apartment the size of my mom's living room. To make the reality even more stunning, I no longer was a 22-year-old single college girl; I was a wife and mother of two. Suddenly not only did this crowded city have no elephants to run free and no wide, open spaces, but even if it had, I would have worried about the safety of such an activity and never would have permitted it. Living in an apartment probably was more sanitary than was living in my imagined hut, but when the roaches visited and the radiators failed to work, even the apartment became a little too primitive for me. The reality of mission life hit hard.

Before I left for the mission field, God had given me a ministry through the radio. I had lived in a town in Arkansas and was known widely for the morning show that I hosted. My background was in communications and speech. I believed that I could talk to just about anyone and relate to people in a meaningful way. I had been to seminary—I knew how to work in the church, how to teach, how to witness. I could see that God was using me and that He had prepared me both for the place I was and for the places I would be going. Then I arrived in Romania.

Speechless

I guess the reality really set in when we got off the plane and I realized that I couldn't talk to anyone. About the only word that made sense to me was *toaleta*. That one I could figure out—especially if I followed my nose. But other than that brief and fleeting knowledge, I was pretty much put out of commission from all communication on a meaningful level.

But shopping—now that was something I was sure I could master! At least I could provide for my family in a meaningful way. Shopping translates in any language, right? Surprise, surprise! In some cultures shopping actually is not a pleasure. In Romania in 1995 all products were behind the counter. I had to ask for them by name. If that wasn't possible, I had to do a lot of pointing. If I didn't actually see the product I needed, then I was in real trouble. Seeing us arrive at the market became the highlight of the locals' days. We imitated chickens, used body language to describe diapers, and played charades to find baking powder. Now, this process seems comical, but at the time it was pretty humiliating. And that was just grocery shopping. I couldn't even take care of the daily necessities with a modicum of dignity.

Sometimes I'd think about the fact that we actually were there to share with people about Jesus, not just to hunt for food. How would I ever be able to do that? First, I couldn't talk to them; secondly, by the time I could talk to them, I would have made such a fool out of myself that they wouldn't listen to me.

Now I admit: a lot of it was pride on my part. Being from a communications background made me feel as though I was a complete failure when I was unable to communicate in an intelligent way. My husband learned more quickly than I. Soon people were choosing to talk to him instead of me because I didn't speak as well. Ouch! And Romanians are very honest people. They would howl with laughter when I made a mistake and ask me things such as, "Why does your husband speak better than you?" I was having to eat a big piece of humble pie; this hurt.

One day I did try to talk to someone about Jesus. I had made friends with a neighbor. She was showing me where the best bread store was. As we walked, I tried to think of a way to talk to her about spiritual stuff. Being the aggressive personality that I am, I jumped in without thinking about how I would continue. I asked her about a healer that had been downtown in the square; I hoped to begin talking about how Jesus was the real healer. I wasn't exactly sure how the conversation would go, but I was desperate to try to do something worthwhile. After about five minutes, I wished that I never had begun that conversation, because I realized that she thought I supported the mystical healer and thought he was from God. I didn't have the vocabulary to explain otherwise and had to just keep saying, "No! I don't believe that!" It was a very frustrating experience. I went home feeling as though I had shamed the Name of Christ instead of honoring Him.

Stay-at-home mom

The second disappointment was that I felt paralyzed by the fact that I was a mother of young children. In the States I could be a stay-at-home mom and still do other things—namely participate in church, because churches are family-friendly. I could attend Bible study and fellowship with other women, because during that time activities were planned for the kids. I could go to Wal-Mart with my kids because the store has great big aisles and buggies. I could let my kids play outside, which had clean grass (no dog poop) and privacy. The list could go on and on. In Romania stay-at-home moms stay at home. Period. During their children's toddler years many national mothers actually stayed away from church, because making their kids sit through 2- to 3-hour serices in a hot, crowded church was difficult. We attended (most of the time), but doing so was tough.

I couldn't take them shopping, because you walk to the store and take home only what you can carry in your two arms. Children can't go outside without you because you live on the fourth floor; playing in the parking lot requires supervision. The reality of what staying home meant was a little overwhelming. I felt as though I could do absolutely nothing of benefit to the mission endeavor as long as my kids were young. Where were those wide-open spaces and good-natured elephants of which I had dreamed? Instead I was confined to an apartment with two kids who had no friends, no television, and, I feared, no future. They didn't look forward to going to church, they couldn't play with friends, they couldn't go out with Mommy to run errands—they couldn't do anything. I felt as though neither they nor I had any life, much less an impact on this culture. If anything, the culture was impacting me—in a big way.

Our brothers in Christ

When we decided to go to Romania, we expected to go work with Christians who desperately desired us to be there and who, under persecution, had been purified. We just knew that they would have a holy aura about them, since they had seen such difficulties and gone through such cleansing. We were some-what surprised to find that sin still reigns—even in Romania.

When we first arrived, we went directly to language school. We were two of four missionaries from our organization in the city; we knew only one Romanian family. We sort-of expected to be shown around and given the royal treatment, since we had traveled so far and given up so much. But the nationals weren't really all that thrilled to meet us until they had some sort of financial need that they supposed we could meet. They didn't understand what we had given up either, because to them we appeared to them still to have a lot—much more than they did. Convincing others that you are suffering is difficult as you drive by in your car while they walk to the bus station.

On one occasion I met the director of a new Christian radio station in the town and thought that maybe I could help the station since I had experience in that area. When I offered, he was thrilled; I thought my contribution to the mission endeavor might begin after all. He took me to the station and showed me around and explained the scope of his vision. I was excited and asked how I might be a part. Immediately he started throwing dollar figures around. I realized that to him my experience and willingness really weren't valued—only my money was. Now don't misunderstand—I know running a radio station takes money. But I had hoped to be a resource in and of myself—to find something to justify my presence. I was disappointed.

To the Romanians America represented money. We could not convince them that money was not our most valuable resource. They felt sure that they understood the mission work there, but they lacked funds. We even had one pastor tell us that sending him the money required to move our family to Romania would have been better than was our traveling there ourselves.

After we got over this initial shock, we dug our heels in and formed relationships with the Christian leaders. We were determined to help them understand our vision for our relationship with them. As we began to understand the workings of the church there, we were shocked to find out that there, just like in America, we didn't like all that we saw.

I'm sure persecution purified the church in some respects. Enough cannot be said for all that devoted Christians sacrificed because they loved God and determined to worship Him despite persecution and pressure from the government. But a mentality under communism seeped into all areas of life, including the church. These were patterns of thinking that were products of a lifetime under a godless government—patterns of which the people themselves weren't even aware. Since we were from outside the circumstances, we could see these patterns clearly. We began to see that things that were survival skills during the communist era were sin without it.

For example church members had had to be secretive about their faith. To worship God they often broke the laws. That mentality remained; a lack of ethics and integrity prevailed because they were accustomed to being deceptive and sneaky and outsmarting the authorities.

Under communism one out of every four people worked for the secret police and reported crimes of the church. Being suspicious of your neighbors and closed to those whom you didn't know was necessary. In the present day that mentality remained. Church members didn't know their neighbors or try to reach them with the gospel; they were cold and distant to others and slow to trust even another brother in Christ.

Under communism the believer stood out from the unbeliever. The believer did not participate in the secular society. A stark division existed between the two worlds. In present day that meant that the world was not welcome in the church. The church became legalistic—requiring certain modes of behavior and dress—to be acceptable. The church failed to welcome a searching nonbeliever because the person didn't fit. Church became the meeting place for the holy and not an evangelistic body at all.

The church was not the only place in which we were disappointed. Among our own missionaries we saw evidence of worldly behavior. I don't know why we would have expected anything different. My husband and I knew we were not the stereotypical holy persons that missionaries always seemed to be. We were just average people who loved God and wanted to obey Him. But when we saw that other missionaries were the same as we were, we were disappointed. They sometimes were thoughtless, driven by the wrong motives, full of self, lacking faith, negative, and on and on. They had not been perfected on the plane trip across the Atlantic any more than we had. Arguments and bad attitudes and lots of need for grace still were present. But somehow we thought that when we entered the mission field, we were entering the holy of holies. To find out otherwise sort of burst our balloon. We still would have to live among the imperfect and find the grace to accept and survive.

So, why did we stay?

So with all these disappointments, why did we stay? We were called—pure and simple. Instead of making us question God's wisdom in sending us, each disappointment made us re-examine our motivation for serving. Were we there to be appreciated and lauded as super-Christians, or were we there to serve God? Were we there to share with the world our wisdom and godliness, or were we willing humbly to continue to learn from Him? Were we there to have adventure and a better life, or were we there to follow Him wherever He would lead us? Were we there to love the lovely or the unlovely? Were we there to work

27

with perfect Christians or with those saved by the grace of God just like we had been? Each situation and each disappointment only worked to purify us and to make us more like Him. Until we became missionaries, we had no idea how much junk was in our hearts. I thought I had developed the fruit of the Spirit, but suddenly all my fruit seemed to be rotting. I began to see that I merely had learned to cope in my society, but when the norms and boundaries were taken away, I wasn't sure how to react. I couldn't rely on what other Christians would do, because I never had known another Christian in this situation. Nothing made sense anymore. Suddenly I dealt with anger, fear, loneliness, and pride in ways I never had before experienced. I didn't even know I was capable of feeling the way I felt. But my control was gone. I was free-falling. I wasn't conditioned to behave to these circumstances. My walk with God took on a whole new dimension as I sought Him constantly for answers. He taught me through each of these disappointments. The situation was uncomfortable, but it was the greatest growing time in my life.

What are your expectations? I encourage you to abandon them now and tell God that you are a blank slate—ready to learn all that He has for you to learn in whatever mode He wants to teach you. If you are like me, you may think that you've been through your training. You are on the mission field now because God already has prepared you. That's exactly what He's been doing for the last few years. Now you are ready to bless others.

I guarantee that the first couple of years will be the most intensive training you've ever had. Nothing can prepare you for what will take place when you get off that plane. Satan doesn't want you there; you will know that. Be ready to learn whatever God has for you to learn; don't fight Him. Determine now to spend quality time studying God's Word, as you make sense of all the emotions, disappointments, and joys. Don't wait until crises hit. Yes, you've been prepared for this time, but that doesn't mean He's through teaching you; it means that you are ready for the next level. Be patient. Learn from Him. Accept the trials and the sorrows; practice finding your joy only in Him.

During the first couple of years I constantly would go to the Lord and ask Him to give me the solution to a problem. *How do I love this person? How do I work with this culture? How do I overcome my fear? How do I accept this humiliation? How do I live with this disappointment?* Every single time the answer from the Lord was the same! *Learn more from Me. Jesus, more of Jesus,* was the answer every time. If I saw things as He did, loved as He did, understood as He did, then everything would be okay. I learned to sit at Jesus' feet and learn of Him.

I never realized this before, but I often had found my joy in other things instead of in Christ Himself. When the other things were stripped away, I began to find joy in Him alone. That was the greatest gift He could have given me. Now, I can take that with me wherever I go, in whatever situation I find myself. I need not fear anything now, because He always is with me and never will forsake me. In Him I find my joy. What a blessing!

QUESTIONS FOR DISCUSSION

1. Describe what you envisioned the "mission field" being like when God first called you to missions.

2. List three ways your answer above differs from the actual circumstances in which you currently serve.

1.
2.
3.

3. Make a list of the expectations you have in the areas:

My ministry
Personal fruit
Living conditions
Host culture

4. Look up the following Scriptures: Write out how each of these relates to the subject of expectations.

Ephesians 2:10

Philippians 2:13

Philippians 4:12-13

Proverbs 16:9

5. Either individually or as a group spend time in prayer and give to the Lord each expectation that you have. Lay it, by name, on the altar and ask Him to remove these from your heart so that you will be able to receive all that He has for you.

Chapter 2

Home Away from Home

Before God put me in Romania, I had read a lot of missionary stories and was under the impression that when one entered another country as a God-called missionary, that country sort-of became like home to the person. The missionary felt as though she belonged to this people group; the love she had for the people was as the love she would have for her own. I thought that meant that it would all "fit." I would be able to rest and say "Okay, I've done it; I've gone where God called me—wow! This feels good!" This break from the first culture and total absorption into the second was something that I thought was a natural part of the missionary call.

Thus I was disappointed when I walked off the plane in 1995 and didn't fall in love with the Romanians or their country. I kept thinking that this would happen—that one day I'd wake up and feel as though I was Romanian. But I finally concluded that I wasn't ever going to become Romanian and that I really didn't want to.

For a long time this bothered me. I continually went to God and asked Him to give me this special kind of love—this belonging, this heart for MY people group. God certainly gave me a burden. I saw the lost; my heart broke. I saw the effects of communism; I wept. I saw their sins; I felt grieved, but I did not love those people as my own.

However, when God began to show us that He wanted us to leave Romania and minister in another country, I started to see how connected I was and how painful leaving would be. And then I realized that God had not told me to attach myself to those people or that place but only to attach myself to Him. He told me to follow Him. When God reminded me of this, my response was "Yeah! But I already did that! That's why I'm here!" God gently reminded me that following Him is not a one-time experience; it is something that is done continually. Again, the tent-pegs had to be removed. I needed to consider moving to another camp-site for a while. Again, I needed to consider taking on another culture. Again, I needed to consider trying to "fit." So, what? Do I abandon the first two cultures and take on a third "as my own"? Are our hearts that shallow? Does God expect that kind of turning aside of the things we hold dear? Of course not! He wants us to wrap our hearts around only one thing—that is Himself.

Snug and comfy

During the months leading up to our appointment to missionary service, I struggled a lot with fear. Fear of the unknown, fear of leaving those I loved, fear for the future of my children, and so on and so on. On one hand I felt prepared to embark on this journey, but on the other I knew that I always would be undeserving of any ministry. I wasn't sure I was ready or good enough for what God had called me to do. During that time God gave me a very special verse to take with me. Ephesians 2:10 says *For we are His workmanship, created in Christ Jesus to do good works, which God prepared in advance for us to do* (NIV). This verse helped me to realize that regardless of how unworthy I was, God had planned on my doing this very thing and made me suitable for it.

But along with the comfort was the false assurance that finally stepping into that work would be the end of the moving and changing and shifting and flexing. I would have arrived and could finally rest—so I thought. No more preparing and looking ahead; no more packing up and feeling temporary in a place or position; no more goodbyes to those I held dear. I would leave the comfort of my present life and take on a new one, which would be even more comfortable, I thought, because it was God's perfect plan for me. I imagined it fitting me like a warm coat on a cold day. I just knew that I would feel all warm and snugly and safe—right in the center of God's will.

I quickly learned that a stagnant life with God really is not possible. Just like your personal devotional life always has to be moving and growing, or it is dying; so the practical steps of following Christ are as well. He doesn't so much call us to one task as to one Taskmaster. Going with Him isn't a one-time experience; it is a way of life.

Following daily

As Christians we learn that we are to follow Christ. We probably all have studied the passage of Scripture stating that we are to take up our crosses daily and follow Him. But somehow we forget the "daily" part and think that following Him is, at best, a one-time deal, or at worst, it will occur in chunks—re-evaluating during those milestones in our lives—marriage, childbirth, graduation, 40th birthday, retirement. But daily means daily.

Look at the children of Israel after they left Egypt. They were to move when the presence of God moved. They had a pillar of fire by night and a cloud by day. God made them to be watching Him constantly.

How often do we re-examine the direction of our lives? Do we go days or weeks or even months or years without being sure of God's presence at all? God didn't require this type of following from the Israelites just because He wanted to keep them guessing. He did it because He knew their natures. He knew how easily they were led astray.

Look what happened when God left them in the valley while Moses went up to receive the Ten Commandments. They immediately fell into sin.

They didn't even purposely say, "Hey, let's sin!" But they had been left alone and took matters into their own hands. They were trying to worship God through the golden calf, but their efforts were a disgrace to God. Isn't that true of us, too? How often do we fail to sense God's presence, so instead of seeking it out or waiting on Him, we begin to take matters into our own hands? We move and change and forge ahead with or without assurance that God is with us. For this reason God made them daily, even hourly, watch the cloud and the fire—so they would not lose focus. They might try to follow God, but they certainly would mess it up.

The same thing was true when the Israelites complained of hunger. God provided. He gave them manna. Not a month's supply so that they could have some assurance that tomorrow was taken care of, but a day's supply. God knew that they needed a daily reminder that they were dependent on Him, so He gave it anew every morning. He does the same for us. Our daily times in the Word and prayer prepare us for the day that's ahead. We can't store up personal time with God and then take a vacation and just rely on the overflow. We have no overflow. God renews us every day.

Beyond our comfort zones

At a recent conference the speaker spoke about going to the edge in our Christian lives. He asked us to define what *the edge* meant. In thinking about that I realized that the edge was right beyond our comfort zones. Our nature is to want to be comfortable. We feel unsettled and vulnerable if we aren't comfortable. We don't want to depend on another for our survival. This is true even if we are speaking of God. We say that we want to follow Him to the ends of the earth, but we want a road map first. We want God to entrust us with the secret plan before we take off. If He refuses, then we often say that we aren't sure that we hear His voice anymore or that He isn't leading in that direction. Could He want you to follow without knowing all the details?

Look at Abraham. He was told to pack up and go to a country that he did not know. God didn't even tell Him where that country was or how many days he would have to travel to get there. Abraham obeyed. He did it. He followed God.

You would think that after he arrived, he could take things easy and relax a little. Abraham was old and had shifted his whole life to obey God's command. Now the time had arrived to get re-established, settled in, and be happy and secure in the fact that he was right in the middle of God's will. He could live out the rest of His life knowing that He had followed God obediently.

But look what God did. He pushed Him to the edge again and asked Him to sacrifice his only son, Isaac. Why did He do this? Did He want to make sure that Abraham was not getting too comfortable in His faith—resting in his own accomplishments or knowledge? Did He just want to torture Abraham? I believe He did this to bless Him. It helped Abraham re-affirm where his trust and security were. They weren't in Isaac. They were in God. They weren't in things being easy. They were in God alone. He never would lose the joy that springs from a heart that is secure and unshakable. As the incident with Isaac shows, no situation that would shake him would occur. His hope was in God alone. God never changes.

Perfect love casts out fear

Another interesting thing to see is that Abraham never doubted God's goodness. This request to sacrifice his son seemed pretty horrible, but Abraham didn't flinch. He knew God intimately enough to know that He is good and whatever He asked Abraham to do was good. Abraham didn't understand why God would command such a thing, but he was able to trust without understanding because of His knowledge of God and God's love for His people. He wasn't afraid because He understood God's nature and was able to entrust his dearest possession—Isaac—into God's care. He knew that God would be faithful to His promise. Abraham even believed that God would raise Isaac from the dead after he was sacrificed in order to keep His promise to multiply Abraham's seed through this promised child.

Most of my fears and hesitations in obedience arise because I have not learned well enough that God is good and that everything He wants to do is good. I have not truly comprehended His love for me. If you think about it, most of our fears center around the things that we hold dear. We don't want to lose what we love. Doing so hurts too much. Maybe the things we love include our families, our material possessions, our children, our status, our health, our lives. We want to hold on—to maintain. Loss scares us. But if we can arrive at the place that we can hold on loosely to everything except for God Himself, then we need never fear, because He never will be taken away from us. He is always for us. Therefore this relationship with God also nullifies the need to worry about those things that we love.

What's really crazy is that often we forget that the very things we hold onto—the very things we are afraid to entrust to God—were given to us by God Himself. They were gifts, just like Isaac was God's miracle gift to Abraham and Sarah. Yet we are afraid to trust Him with them. We want to cling. This is our nature. God knows this and so constantly practices prying things loose from us to help us learn to cling only to Him. He knows that only then will we have joy; only then will fear not have power over us.

The Word says that perfect love casts out fear. When we can love Him perfectly and understand perfectly His love for us, then we never will fear again. This is part of that process. Love Him above all other things, but also learn to trust in His love for us. It is perfect; in it is nothing to fear. How often do we find ourselves hoping that God won't do something that will cause pain to us? We don't want to pray for God's will to be done, because we are afraid that we don't like what He wants to do. We don't seem to understand that all that God does is good. All of it springs from His perfect love. We really don't trust Him, do we?

When I was in high school, a popular song was entitled "Hold on Loosely." This tune often pops into my head when I am reminding myself that we are not to hold on to anything on this earth too tightly—not our families, homes, friends, children—even our own lives. That's what Jesus means when He tells the disciples to hate their own mothers and fathers in comparison to their love for Him. He, and only He, is constant, steady, stable, secure. Follow Him—not a vision or a mission or a heart burden. If we follow anything other than Him, then we begin to lose our focus; the thing we are following becomes a replacement for Him—an idol.

But what would THEY say?

In today's society following like Abraham did would be ridiculed. It would be seen as irresponsible—flighty. We have been taught to be cautious—to look out for our own best interests.

Recently I talked to a friend of mine who was put in a position of readjusting her whole life—again. This was very stressful for her. She was struggling with the reality of uprooting her whole family and having to be unsettled again. Her biggest problem, she thought, was not with God but with the human element through whom she received the request to move. She thought the request was unfair. She was a little angry with the leadership for making her and her family change their whole life around.

I asked her a question to which I have given much thought. When do we just accept what has been dealt us and rejoice that God is sovereign over the events of our lives? When do we raise a fist of defiance and fight for our own interests? Her response, in the midst of the pain, was that whenever she was asked to do something that disrupted her family life, then for the good of her family she had a right to complain. I thought about that a long time. Something about it didn't ring true. Didn't sacrificing Isaac disrupt Abraham's family life? Yet it was the request of God.

Our society teaches us that following God to this extreme is irresponsible. We need balanced lives, not extremism. We avoid endangering our children or being irresponsible by foolishly following a call or compromising their educations or making their lives stressful. I can't help thinking that being tied up and placed on an altar may have been a little stressful for Isaac. Yet the Bible doesn't mention Isaac needing extensive counseling later because his father obeyed God. Did you know that some grandparents have filed lawsuits against their children for irresponsible parenting in taking their grandchildren to the mission field? The society in which we live worships health, fitness, cleanliness, beauty, wealth, and convenience; to choose to put our commitment to obey God ahead of the "needs" of ourselves and our children seems absurd and negligent in such a context.

Jesus Himself is our example in this. He willingly subjected Himself to a physical life that was destined for suffering and death (and resurrection!) so that He might accomplish salvation for us. The prophets were called to do all sorts of crazy things that made them look as though they were fools and probably were not very good for their health in order to speak to the people of Israel in word pictures. They obeyed because the call of God was on their lives. Hosea remained faithful to an unfaithful wife because God told him to do so. John the Baptist didn't maintain a good diet or standard of living, yet He specially was chosen by God to do just that. Jesus taught His disciples that their lives probably would end in a violent way; yet they took their families along with them (1 Cor. 9:5) and followed Jesus' example of obedience until death. God's concern over physical safety simply is not what ours is. He is much more concerned with our spiritual well-being.

The world may not agree with us if we refuse to cling to the things of this world. Actually even your moms might not agree. But God's word is clear that this is the only way to follow Christ.

What about you?

So finally I realized that I had not become Romanian because God never asked me to do so. What He does ask of me is to acknowledge first and foremost that I am a child of the King and my citizenship is in heaven, not on earth. In the promise of heaven I have found my security. In the King of heaven I have found the One I can love as my own. At the Throne of heaven I can unpack my bags and rest forever. I'm glad God kept me from completely taking on a second culture as my own. I've learned from it, grown through it, and see myself more clearly because of it, but this is neither my culture nor my people. As Christians, we are to transcend our cultures and live as if we belong to another one altogether. As a missionary, that truth is only made clearer. As I belong to many, I easily see that I really belong to none, but my belonging is in heaven. It will determine who I am and whom I love and what I sound like. It is my culture and my home. It does transcend all the other cultures I will pass through on this earth.

When I realized this truth, I felt good, because I already had been through many "homes." What God was showing me seemed to tie all the loose ends together. However I realize that you may be reading this from the front end and find no comfort in these truths. Maybe you are waiting for the time in which you finally can get settled somewhere. If you're like me, for sometime you've known that God called you to be a missionary, but the process of getting to the mission field has taken years, so for a long time you have been waiting for this moment. It is the fulfillment of many years of planning, dreaming, preparing, praying, and waiting—waiting to finally "arrive" at your destined place of service.

God may have one place for you to go. When you reach that destination, you will have a sense of rightness that assures you that you are to remain with these people for a long time to come. Quite possibly God did not give me that belonging because He knew that I wouldn't remain my whole life in that place and I didn't need to belong there. Perhaps one day I will feel that "fit" that means I am to settle where I am. But even though some of the lessons God has been teaching me were for me alone, in my situation, some of them were eternal truths. These I want to share with you. Even if one day I physically do settle in somewhere, I still want daily to ask God what He has for me. I want moment by moment to be watching for His presence. I never want to cling to what He gives me but instead to hold on to the giver. I always want to trust Him and remain willing to go wherever He says to go. I want to know Him well enough that I trust His goodness and His love. This has to be the cry of our hearts. Let Him be your all in all.

QUESTIONS FOR DISCUSSION

1. Share with your small group the "burden" you have for your target people group. How do you envision connecting with the people in this group?

2. Read Ephesians 2:10. Discuss how this verse impacts your understanding of your call.

3. Read Philippians 1:21. Discuss the difference between being called to a task and being called to a taskmaster.

4. Discuss the practical steps involved in following Christ daily. Then discuss some of the obstacles and the obstacle-overcomers that you personally have discovered in your daily walk. Lastly discuss the dangers of failing to follow daily.

5. Discuss the impact on your fears and hesitations to obedience that understanding God's perfect love would have.

Spend time in prayer asking God
• to help you give up your own ideas about home and security, and
• to help you find your home in Him alone.

Chapter 3

Near to the Source

One thing I really like about being a missionary is that I'm forced, more or less, to live beyond my coping capacity. I'm convinced that what is wrong with many churches and the people in them is that they have set up their lives so that they can cope without anyone's help—even God's. When I left America for the mission field, I no longer was able to cope with the life I had chosen. It was a bit beyond me. It has forced me to rely on God in a way that I never have previously. Though the trials sometimes are greater, my knowledge of Him and intimacy with Him are greater as well, because the trial made me rely on Him in a way I never had done previously.

When we grow up hearing about God and from childhood understanding that He wants us to read His Word and pray, such practices often become habitual. As we grow up, our lives fill with so many other things that are vying for our attentions that often the basics that as children we learned get crowded out. In the book of Deuteronomy, God tells His people. *"These commandments that I give you today are to be upon your hearts. Impress them on your children. Talk about them when you sit at home and when you walk along the road, when you lie down and when you get up. Tie them as symbols on your hands and bind them on your foreheads. Write them on the doorframes of your houses and on your gates"* (Deut 6:6-9, NIV).

Unfortunately what we often learn is not the totality of single-mindedness that God seems to want. We learn the minimum requirements. We learn to give at least 15 minutes a day—preferably at sunrise—to the Lord. We learn to pray at every meal and before we go to bed. We learn church lingo to describe our circumstances. And that's where it ends. The words in Deuteronomy express God's desire for us to love His Word. He wants our lives to be wrapped around it. He is not telling His people to put up wall plaques from the local Christian bookstore and wear WWJD bracelets. He is telling them to make His words the focus of their lives. Do you know what that means?

That means that the house in which you live is yours because that is the house with which you best can glorify God. That means that the way you speak is not dictated by the situation but by the River of Living Water flowing from within you. That means that the way you dress is not determined by the latest fashion trend but by your desire to represent Christ wherever you go. That means that God's words and His laws are not merely the focus of the couple of hours on Sunday when you are at church, but they constantly are on your mind and in your thoughts and on your tongue. That means that when your children have questions about the problems they face, your advice doesn't echo the latest psychobabble that is popular, but it reflects your relationship with God and your absolute belief that His Word has the answers to all of life's challenges. That means that you have no circumstances in your life that are not ordained by God. You know this because you see your days through His perspective. This is the kind of impact God wants His Word to have in our lives. He wants us to love It, to live It, to breathe It.

One day I was talking to a friend about a teacher at my son's school. This teacher is a very sincere believer and talks a lot about God. Immediately you can tell that God is the focus of her life and not just a pastime. My friend commented that the teacher seemed different. I agreed, as I thought about the obvious way in which she transparently loved God and His Word. But that's not what my friend meant. Her impression was that the teacher was weird and was too showy about her Christianity. She saw that the woman brought God into every subject she discussed. My friend believed this was inappropriate. This struck me as odd, since my friend is a sincere Christian as well. But the current trend in Christianity is that we are to be balanced in our daily walk—not too extreme nor offensive, not too radical, and not "Christian" in a way that would make others uncomfortable around us. We are, after all, to be an aroma of Christ, right? So we don't want to be offensive. We are to blend. We are to make Christianity palatable and attractive to the world.

Unfortunately this trend is not biblical. According to the Bible we are to be radical in our faith. We are not to seek the approval of people but of God. An old saying goes, "We should not be so heavenly minded that we are no earthly good." Quite frankly that is not possible. If we are truly focused on God and His Word, then He will use us as He wishes. The results will be infinitely greater than will anything we can imagine. The foundational Scripture for this book, 2 Corinthians 2:14-15, says, *But thanks be to God, who always leads us in triumphal procession in Christ and through us spreads everywhere the fragrance of the knowledge of him* (NIV). God is doing the leading; God is doing the spreading; the knowledge of Him is fragrant. It's all extremely God-centered.

A good example of this is Ananias and Sapphira in the New Testament (Acts 5). They had some money and wanted to be good Christians and give God some of the money but not all of it. Still they weren't bad people. They just wanted to take care of a few pressing needs—maybe take a vacation. They were proud of themselves for putting God first and only leaving a little for themselves. But God wasn't pleased with them. In fact He was so displeased that He struck them dead. Why was God so harsh for such a little thing? For one reason through this He showed us how seriously He takes sin—what a severe matter dishonoring God really is and how much grace He usually shows us in restraining judgment for our sins. Even the slightest slip deserves the same punishment as Ananias and Sapphira had, but He is merciful. He wasn't unjust in His treatment of these two. He exercised justice. Normally He exercises mercy.

Another reason is that we see here an example of what God desires of us. He doesn't want half of what we have—what we are. He wants it all, whether it's money or possessions or time or love or service. When we become His children, these things are given over to His control. They claimed to be giving all to Him but really were keeping some back for themselves. This represented lying to the Holy Spirit. How many of us are guilty of the same thing? We say that our lives belong to God, but we have put limits on what God can ask us to do.

When I heeded the call to missions and moved away to another country, I believed that I was giving all I had to God. I don't know what I expected when I reached the other side of the ocean. Maybe I thought that this was the big sacrifice and from that point on I never would struggle with giving it all to God again. I was surprised to find out that it was just the beginning. He didn't just want my career choice; He wanted my days, nights, and hours. He wanted to infiltrate every square-inch of my life. And He didn't do this to hurt me or because He is mean and selfish and egotistical. He did it because He knows that this is the very thing for which He created us. Only in Him will we ever be complete. He wants for us what we need most—what will fulfill our very purpose in creation. So He patiently and steadily works on us until we are all His.

Growing pains

One way God works on us is putting us in situations that stretch us. In moving to another culture I've experienced many times when I felt stretched beyond my ability to cope. All of the rules had changed; I was left with no road map to follow. I had God; that was all, but He was enough. To survive I had to stay near to the Source.

Beggars

When we visited Romania in 1991, we noticed that beggars were on the street. I was not used to seeing a lot of beggars; this unnerved me. I felt so sorry for these people and couldn't imagine living at that level of society and being at the mercy of others for help. How humiliating it must be! How sad for them!

Then I moved to Romania; beggars became a part of our lives. My sentiments quickly changed as I watched how they operated, learned about their mafia type set-up, over and over again experienced their bald-faced lies. No longer did I feel pity for them; I hated them. I became very angry with them as they appeared at my door and wouldn't leave even if I pretended not to be home. I felt threatened, stalked, targeted. If you had told me that I could feel this way about another person, I wouldn't have believed you. But these people had encroached on my space and my right to privacy in a way no one else ever had; I didn't know how to deal with it. Suddenly "love those who curse you" and "give to those who ask" took on a whole new meaning. I had no idea what to do with these people. I also remembered the biblical imperative, "Don't cast your pearls before swine," and "be wise as serpents, innocent as doves."

Neighbors

The same kind of confusion took place with my neighbors. The only way I knew to love others was by opening my heart to them and showing them some measure of trust. I had a neighbor who bothered me from the first day we moved in. She was young and had a baby. Although I wished that we could be friends, she didn't seem to view me as that. She constantly asked for our things and pushed her company on us in an obtrusive way. She pretended a familiarity with us that we really didn't have. And she lied repeatedly.

Many times I tried to share Christ with her, but she had a lack of understanding that I couldn't pinpoint. After our family returned from our Stateside assignment, my relationship with this woman changed. She seemed more trustworthy and sincere. I was able to lead her to Christ; we became friends. She started helping me around the house and as a babysitter. I began to trust her and often left her alone in the house. I was very happy with our friendship.

After a few months, though, we started missing some money. We always tried to find another reason, but the fact was that she was stealing from us. This was tough for me to believe. I was deeply saddened by the loss of that friendship.

After that I wasn't sure how I could show love to her. I wasn't angry, but we could have no reconciliation because she wouldn't admit that she had done it. I became more suspicious of people and tried to be more careful. But I couldn't figure out how to show love to people I couldn't trust.

I never realized before how in my own mind the two were intertwined. God reminded me of John 2:24-25. This passage says that Jesus did not put His trust in people, because He knew what is in people. He could say this, yet we know that He loved us perfectly. So I knew a way existed; I just had to learn it. My whole idea of love needed to be revamped.

Communications

Communicating with the public at large also left me wondering. If I was polite and nice, I got nothing accomplished. The Romanians are very Latin in nature, which means that they are exuberant, lively, animated, and vocal. If I was polite and expected to be treated with respect, I got run over and was shown no respect. To get respect I had to be pushy, loud, argumentative, and assertive. This seemed as though it was a good thing, because by nature I am this way anyway. I quickly took to waving my arms at people in traffic and honking my horn. I enjoyed being in a place in which to get my way, I had to speak my mind and debate with people. At first I felt odd expressing myself in this way—to unleash the fury within and be praised for it, but I quickly became accustomed to it. One day we were in a shopping area and stopped to buy some lunch. I had let my son, David, and his friend order their own lunch and pay. When it was ready, I went back to pick up their order. But I didn't have the receipt for what the boys had bought because the they mistakenly had thrown it away. I explained this to the man at the counter, but he promptly put my food down just out of my reach, shrugged his shoulders, and turned around to help another customer. I couldn't believe he was going to deny me the food just because I didn't have the receipt. He knew that the boys were with me. He knew they had paid for the food. But he refused to give me the food without the ticket. I became outraged and began yelling at him and waving my arms, just like the Romanians do. I held my ground, didn't give in, acted as though I had no class at all, and got my food. I then I realized that I was enjoying myself too much.

One big difference between the Romanians and me is that when they wave their hands and speak loudly and harshly, they aren't necessarily angry. That is just the way they express themselves. For me to act that way, I had to get really mad; I had to get in the flesh. But walking in the flesh is not part of the culture of Christ. I wasn't sure how to handle this dichotomy. God doesn't care if we have a rough exterior; what He cares about is the heart. So I was faced with the problem of how to communicate effectively in a way that would glorify God.

Anger

A common emotion with which missionaries deal is anger. Maybe it's being in a situation in which you feel out of control and can't make yourself understood, or maybe it's just the fact that things don't make sense anymore. Whatever the case, just about every missionary I have known has been surprised to find out how much rage was inside. The same was true with me. I'd get on the road in traffic with no rules and crooked cops and would be emotionally exhausted by the time I got home. I was surprised how quickly my day could be ruined just because of another person in a hurry. I had never thought of myself as someone with a temper. I didn't know how to control it, because I never had had that problem before.

One time two of my colleagues and I drove two hours to go to a K-mart that had opened in Eastern Europe. Never did I think I would travel two hours to shop at a K-mart, but the mission field will do strange things to you. As we arrived and pulled into the parking lot, we found it very crowded. Parking spaces were few and far between. Finally Peggy, the driver, found one; we began to pull in. At that moment a man emerged from the other direction and started to swerve into the same space we were pulling into. I became furious. I had no idea that that sort of anger was in my heart. Before I knew what I was doing, I had jumped out of the car and began beating on this man's car and yelling at him that he had no right to take our place. Peggy and my other colleague were stunned and didn't know whether to commit me or pray for me. The man did move, but only later did I understand that he was not trying to park anyway. He was just trying to turn around so that he could leave. I was so ashamed.

Unmet expectations

One of the toughest things about moving to a new place with a new boss and new rules is that often we enter with expectations that lead to a feeling of entitlement. Many missionaries move onto the field knowing that they have laid their lives at God's feet; whatever occurs is given from His hand. They are willing to live and rear children in less than perfect conditions because they have released their expectations. These missionaries are a joy to work alongside. Others, however, arrive full of expectations and a sense of entitlement to having the things they think they need to survive. This inflexible attitude of demand is a scourge to the missionary community. It breeds discontentment among other missionaries and takes the focus off of the reason for being a missionary in the first place. It isn't about what kind of house you live in or what kind of transportation you use; it's about reaching people for Christ. As a Christian and as a missionary you have given up your rights. *For we who live are constantly being delivered over to death for Jesus' sake, so that the life of Jesus also may be manifested in our mortal flesh* (2 Cor. 4:11).

This feeling of entitlement is especially evident where schools are concerned. Many folks arriving on the field think, "In no way would I put my children in a national school. They are so far behind us" or "Who knows what might happen to her?" Our family has done most varieties—some

Homeschooling, local MK (missionary kid) schools, national schools, and private international schools. We have had good and bad experiences in all of them, but the bottom line is that they are in God's hands. Any of those choices CAN work. When you said "yes" to the mission field, you said "no" to satisfying your own preferences, even if it's for your kids' sake.

Others who struggle with this are people who transfer from one field to another or from one organization to another. They often arrive in their new home full of expectations of which they are often not even aware. These folks do not realize they have a process of adjustment to go through—even a kind of culture shock. This is true whether the departure from the previous situation was positive or negative. They also inevitably compare the present to the past. They make remarks such as, "In Africa, it was this way . . .." "In Brazil our leaders always . . .." "In the Philippines we had . . .." In good *Wizard of Oz* fashion, new team members sometimes want to grab them by the collar and say, "You are not in Kansas anymore, Toto!"

Ultimately the more open you are to the things God has in your future, the easier time you will have accepting the unexpected. When we first were in our orientation to prepare us for the field, our leaders told us that you not only have to be flexible as missionaries, you have to be fluid. I can attest that this is true. The quicker you allow God to melt away your preconceived ideas and expectations, the happier you'll be.

Conclusion

These situations and others like them led me to get on my face before God in a way I never had done before. Quiet times no longer amounted to a luxury; they represented a survival skill. I no longer couldn't find time to pray; I lived in prayer. I knew that if God didn't help me through this day, I would go home on the next plane. I was pushed way beyond my limits and way beyond my comfort zone. My coping mechanism was useless. All the rules seemed to be changed; I had to learn how to walk in the Spirit again.

Wow! What an opportunity this was. Often we lose our first love because we lose the joy of our salvation. By having to relearn the basics, I learned them better. It renewed my love and dependency on God. Where many people are getting stale in their walk with God, I was getting a fresh wind. As painful as this was, knowing God in this way was worth everything.

But I didn't realize that I was setting myself up for such a difficult climb. Rarely do we meet anyone who, on purpose, pushes the limit of his or her own comfort zone. By contrast most people spend their whole lives trying to reach and maintain a certain level of comfort. That is their goal. Thus the things that absorb them are things that will help them reach that end. They want to get comfortable, settle down, find their niche. They want to answer all the important questions and figure out where they stand on things and then stash them away for good measure.

Even in following God's call to the mission field, I suppose I was looking for that spiritual rest that I thought would arrive with obedience. I wanted to find God's will for me and then settle in for the long haul.

But getting comfortable often can lead to spiritual drowsiness. God never told us to seek this kind of life. Yes, we are to rest in Him, but that is rest from striving and worrying. The Word tells us that we are to run the race as those who want to win! (1 Cor. 9:24-26). We are constantly to be in training to run in such a way as to win the prize. The prize isn't salvation. If it were, Paul wouldn't have been running for it after his conversion. So the race shouldn't slow down the longer we know

Jesus. It should heat up as we head toward the finish line. We are to be buffeting our body and exercising our spiritual muscles until God declares the race over. Then we can rest.

A man in his 80s was part of a volunteer team that traveled to Romania one summer. Since his retirement he had been on countless trips as a volunteer. He hoped that until his death, he would continue serving God. He refused to lie down and retire from God's service. While in Romania that summer, this volunteer died. His wife said that nothing would have made him happier than would dying while he was doing the thing he loved the most. He is a good example of not slowing down in his last lap but of running to win the race.

This type of running isn't possible on an empty tank of gas, though. Draw near to God, the Source of all that we need, in order to finish well. Second Peter 1:3 (NIV) says. *His divine power has given us everything we need for life and godliness through our knowledge of him . . ..* We have everything we need at our disposal, but we often fail to tap into the Source.

QUESTIONS FOR DISCUSSION

1. Evaluate your own life by asking yourself how you are living in relation to your coping capacity. Do the things you can do on your own or the things you only can do with God's help determine your life?

2. The only way we can begin to be single-minded in our devotion to God is by establishing good habits. Discuss how we can strive to be single-minded while we safeguard against merely fulfilling the minimum requirements.

3. Discuss the difference between spiritual drowsiness brought on by being too comfortable and the rest that occurs from not worrying and striving.

4. Think through some of the challenges that you currently face or that you may face in the near future that will cause you to draw near to the Source. Pray through these and accept them as God's perfect will for you.

5. Commit to spend time in God's Word and in prayer. Ask God to help you make it your first priority and love and not just a meaningless routine.

Chapter 4

Partnering with Your Husband

When I first fell in love with my husband, I knew we were going to be missionaries—not because he wanted to be a missionary, but because we both were committed to the call God had placed on our lives. We knew that God was leading us in that direction; we were determined to follow. We definitely were partners in this. During the first few years of marriage all that we did involved working toward the goal of going overseas. I finished my seminary degree; he finished his doctorate. While he was a pastor, I worked part-time to help support us. We both reared our two little gifts from God. We rented instead of buying and didn't invest in furniture. We knew that as soon as God said, "Go", we would go. We were a team.

As we prepared to go to Romania, our sending organization interviewed us extensively. Beyond a shadow of a doubt we proved that I, as the wife, was not merely following my husband's call, but I had been called as well. That call was personal and concrete for me. I was not a tag-a-long. I was a missionary.

But when we arrived in Romania, the picture changed. Suddenly, regardless of the Stateside exhortations about us both being missionaries, I definitely felt as though I were the least-important of the two of us and as though I really was just there because of my husband. Yes, I was a good, submissive wife, but the ministry part was in his hands. I even had an overnight guest say to me once that he was sure that the decision to be a missionary wasn't a big deal for me, since I just followed my husband and his decisions. I politely explained to him that was not the way things were, but the reality seemed to be that I really wasn't all that important.

Even in my own mind the mission field was not as I had pictured it. When God called me to be a missionary, I was 22 and single. Of course I did realize that when we actually became missionaries, I was married with children, but I never had reconciled my picture of what a missionary did with the reality of being a wife and mom. Diligently as I tried, once we arrived in Romania, I really couldn't even find the time to be more than that, because life just took more time in a foreign country. Just surviving from one day to the next seemed to zap all my energy.

I tried and tried to find my niche and to find out why God had brought me to Romania if I only was to be a mother and wife. Not that this act wasn't noble enough in itself. It was just that in the States, I was so much better at those things. Why would God bring me to Romania to do these things if He didn't have some other reason? Instead of my personal call being helpful in sorting this out, it actually was part of the problem. I knew that the call had been for me; I knew that God personally wanted me to be in that country. I assumed that it was for a reason. I wanted to know what that reason was. So I kept trying to find something that was unique to me—that matched my talents and abilities—in which I could invest my extra time. Often I would have people ask me, "So what do YOU do?" I would just cringe as I tried to wrestle with a feeling of being inferior.

I'm not sure when it began, but gradually God began to show me that I wasn't really in Romania to do any task, per se, I was there because that's where He told me to go. As much as I hated to admit it, I could tell that at that point God was doing more work in me than through me. This is not always so, but often that inward pruning IS God's purpose.

In my case, it was definitely God's purpose. Every time I tried to show God that I was ready to go to work, He stopped me. Whether with circumstances, failures, sickness—whatever

He wanted to use, I was in an extensive workshop in how to stop and be quiet and listen to God. When God spoke, I wasn't all that excited about what He had to say.

In a Bible study where I was involved, we took a hiatus from our study of Luke to study the role of a woman. This was our leader's idea. Frankly, for several reasons, I dreaded it. One, I felt as though it all was stuff I'd heard a million times before and didn't want to rehash it. Two, I hate the way most books categorize the psyches of men and women, because more times than not, I don't "fit" into the typical woman's category. I begin to wonder whether something is wrong with me or whether the writer really is dumb enough to believe that all women are the same. And three, usually studies on this topic result in a bunch of women sitting around badmouthing their husbands, regretting their own mistakes, and whining about their lives in general. I wanted no part in it.

As things turned out, though, God had a few new insights for me—a few new things that needed to be learned or re-learned. Yes, once again the issues were the same, but my perspective was different; thus different things stood out to me. Yes, once again the authors we considered told me that men were the only ones that were goal-oriented and used the word *cheerleader* when describing my vital contributions to the marriage. And yes, many women were there with many needs, but we kept away from husband-bashing and focused on real issues and how God's Word responds to those issues. Overall it was a great few weeks and it helped me to re-focus on Preston and on my role as his helper, partner, lover, and friend.

The study revealed this significant point: we generally think of wives and mothers in two ways. One is the image of how things used to be—the Ozzie and Harriet days that were lost to the '60s. The other is the woman of today. We know that the present picture lacks a biblical perspective, but often we think that a godly wife resembles the former. However both images are wrong; neither is biblical.

On the same hand our ideas of submission are shaped by our culture. I know of no culture in which the term *submission* is viewed as positive. It has been redefined since biblical times and now at its best conjures up ugly images of passive women and at its worst images of abused ones. However the godly wife that we see in Scripture is anything but a docile patsy. In Proverbs 31 she is strong and directed and capable; in Song of Songs she is an exquisite lover; in the examples of Rahab, Esther, Mary (the mother of Jesus), and Elizabeth she is used of God. As with Elizabeth and Abigail the godly wife sometimes is more sensitive to the Lord's voice than is her husband; as with Joanna she sometimes follows Jesus apart from her husband; as with Priscilla she is praised by Paul as a worker for the Lord; and the list could go on and on.

As I was reading the passages about my role, I realized that I inwardly cringed whenever I got to the word *submission*. I began to understand that I did this because I still think of the matter in the wrong way. If you tell me to submit to God, I don't flinch and rather wholeheartedly agree. But if you tell me to submit to my husband, ugly images immediately flash before my eyes. I know I'm supposed to submit, but the task as I see it is not a pleasant one. And I've never been sure how it fits with my personality—strong, independent, assertive. The waters got muddier when I married Preston, because he is a mild-mannered, phlegmatic, low-key servant. Instead of being able to celebrate the differences that drew us to each other, I made his good qualities look like weaknesses; he made mine look overbearing. This was the crux of a struggle that had gone on for years. I learned that I entered marriage with an unbalanced picture of a godly wife. I didn't like the image I had conjured up and wasn't sure how to reconcile it to who I was.

The Bible study had given me a larger picture and continued the process of freeing me up to be who God created me to be. One key thing that we talked about was how my ROLE wasn't submission. That was my response to his role (required whether he fulfills his role or not). My ROLE is that of a husband-lover. The Bible never tells my husband to force me to submit; that is a voluntary behavior that I am to choose freely. God created us in His image. The man takes on the authoritative leader part of His image; the woman takes on the helper part of His image. Did you know that the word used for *helper* is the same word used throughout the Bible for God Himself? How can that be secondary if God refers to himself in the same way? Ladies, our husbands need us. They were incomplete and unsatisfied without us. God saw that they needed more; they needed help. We were made just for that. We do not need our husbands in the same way they need us. He cannot, by nature, fulfill his God-given tasks without us. God recognized this and didn't fault the man for it but gave him the help he needed. If I fail to understand my husband's need of me and instead compete with him for equal recognition, then we do both of us a disservice and do not honor God. Realizing these truths, I was re-energized to serve my husband with joy.

During this study I also realized how much of my ongoing problems with roles was linked to my relationship with my husband. I felt as though our missionary service was geared toward him and his gifts. I wanted to play a part, too. I found myself disappointed at the prospect of being the support for a ministry that was unique only to him. I had expected to have a ministry unique to me as well; "cheerleader" didn't fit who I was. Finally through this study I began to understand my role as a team member on a team that not only was unique but that also couldn't function without my contribution Preston was unable to do his God-given task without my help.

I'm not saying that I do all the house and kid stuff and he has all the mission experiences. The team concept goes both ways. Preston seemed to understand this better than I. When we lived in Arkansas, I was privileged to have a citywide ministry. Every morning from 5 to 9 a.m. I hosted a morning show on the Christian radio station. During those morning hours Preston stayed home and did the breakfast routine with the kids while I worked. I got home mid-morning; he was free to do the work involved in being a pastor. He also held down another part-time job. He stayed up late with crying babies so that I could sleep and get up at 5 every morning. We were a team. In Romania the primary ministry was his; I had to learn how to be in the helper mode and to see it as a God-given task.

Not all missionary women will be in this position. An older couple who worked with us had grown children; thus this husband and wife did most things together. In our case though, this wasn't possible. I had to embrace being the supporter. I had to begin to understand the value of that. And as I did, God began to show me how much Preston needed me and how his ministry— our ministry—God's ministry—suffered if I didn't do my part. He needed an orderly home; he needed happy children who were well-adjusted; he needed meals and shopping done. He needed good family relationships with the neighbors. If I didn't do those things, then he couldn't do the things he needed to do. I wasn't inferior; I was a necessity. I had to accept the fact that God Himself had the title *helper*. This was nothing to belittle.

After a couple of years an opportunity arose for me to help some students with a radio station. The times I would go and meet with them, Preston took over for supper and bedtime. We worked as a team. But during the time I failed to understand his need of me and the importance of being a helper, I hurt our impact a great deal. I failed to undergird Preston as I was supposed to do and made him weaker by that.

When we moved to Prague, my role changed even more. The kids were older; everyone was in school. I was asked to be a part of the media team at our regional office. Preston and the kids remained my number-one priority, but God provided an outlet for me to use the skills and talents He gave me to honor Him. I'm sure in later years, my role will change yet again.

Now when people say, "So what do YOU do?" I tell them— loud and clear! I do whatever God puts before me to do. I love and cherish and care for my family; I pray; I try to make a home that is sweet with the fragrance of Christ; I love my husband, and I do whatever else the Lord brings my way to do. I serve Him faithfully.

The amazing thing is that once I accepted this as being from God, I began to love it a great deal. I no longer judged myself from someone else's standard. I judged myself according to God's Word and according to the smile on my husband's face. He actually did need a cheerleader and not a quarterback. But he is a cheerleader, too.

The roles are not poured into concrete. They are different for every couple. Your roles will be unique to your marriage. I still think that most marriage studies generalize way too much. I am not the typical "cheerleader" type; Preston is not the macho sports fan (until the NCAA basketball tournament!). But we are very different from each other. We need each other very much.

God began to show me how Preston cannot function when he has noise around him. I can write and think and concentrate just fine with a circus going on in my house; he is not capable of this. I can work on my writing in the midst of the hubbub at home. He cannot. He needs quiet and peace. I need to help him find this atmosphere so that he can accomplish what needs to be done.

I don't function in the morning. To wake me Preston gets up and brings me coffee in bed. Then I take care of getting the kids off to school, because the myriad of little things that need to be done drive him crazy, but once I'm awake, they are no problem for me. The list could go on and on. Yours will look different from mine. We had to learn what each other needed and partner together to meet the other's needs. Preston doesn't try to change who I am. He doesn't try to make me into a morning person; I don't try to keep him awake when he's tired. We have learned to accept who the other is and work with what we have.

Someone recently asked me how I knew Preston was the right person for me. I said that I had two criteria. One was that I realized when I met him, I couldn't live without him. Someone wisely told me before I got married, "If you can live without him, DO!" I realized that God intended for us to be together. To do otherwise would have been second-best for both of us. The other thing was that Preston made me a better person. Every other relationship I had had detracted from who I was. With Preston I was complete. He felt the same way. Sometimes after the vows one easily forgets that you once felt that way, but God can help you rediscover His purpose in putting you together.

Remember that the reasons He put you together is not separate from the ministry he called you to perform. Just as He knows that you need each other to be complete, He knows that you both need to participate in order for your ministry to be complete. He didn't call one of you; He called both of you. If you have children, He called you as a family. Each family member has a vital role to play.

Saying these things is easy, but often what keeps us from enjoying the role God has for us is that we are plagued with worry and guilt. We worry that we might not be doing all that God wants us to do; we feel guilty for the same reason. This is Satan's biggest weapon in his fight against us. He cannot rob us of our salvation, but he can certainly take away the joy with which we live it. With confidence and excitement tell those who ask what you do that you follow God's call daily, whatever that may mean for you.

If you're a mother, then mother with God's blessings and with His glory as your goal. If you are a wife, then love your husband in a way that honors God. If He has given you a specific job, then the question is easier to answer, but still you need to verify daily whether you are doing the job for the right reasons. If not you will find your joy ebbing away.

God doesn't need us to get the job done, but He chooses to let us partner with Him so that we can partake of the joy and thrill. Don't let Satan steal that thrill away through worrying that you're somehow disappointing God and not doing enough for Him. God is big enough and His voice is loud enough that He can make you understand what He wants of you. You're not going to miss it—especially not if you are staying in His Word and truly desiring to serve Him. As His child you won't and can't live for long in abject disobedience to Him. Trust Him to use you as He wants to and enjoy the role He has given you to play.

I'm impressed by what the Gospel of Luke says about Mary, the mother of Jesus. Her faith and her responses to God are humble and grateful. Luke 1:38 NKVJ records her response when the angel told her that she would bear a son, Jesus: *"Behold the Lord's bond slave, be it done unto me according to Thy Word."* I just love that. No questioning, whining, griping—not even a false humility—just submission, obedience.

And her song of praise testifies to the fact that she did not think much of the inconvenience this pregnancy was going to cause her. She was focused on God, on His glory, on His awesome plan in which she was privileged to participate.

I also love the fact that after the birth, in the midst of all the craziness—the shepherds arriving to worship, the wise men bringing gifts, the birth itself—Luke 2:19 says that she *treas-*

ured up all these things, pondering them in her heart. She was pondering. I just get a picture of a graceful woman with a peaceful heart, at rest before God, enjoying the strange task to which He had called her and watching with fascination as God fulfilled His plan through her and around her. I want to respond to God like that. I want to ponder instead of frantically looking for answers. I want to praise Him because I know Him and His character and trust what He wants to do in my life even if I don't fully understand it. I want to bow my knee in submission to whatever He calls me to do. She was just a peasant woman— poor and regular—but God saw her heart and chose her to be the channel through whom salvation was brought to the world.

I see a parallel there with us. If our hearts are pure before Him and we respond to His call on our lives, He will use us as a channel to bring salvation to those around us and to the ends of the earth. Pretty great, huh?

QUESTIONS FOR DISCUSSION

1. In your imagination, what does a *husband-lover* look like? In your own marriage how would this concept apply?

2. In order for you and your husband to accomplish the task set before you, functioning as a team is important. Answer the following questions:

a. For the next year, what are your three main goals as a couple?

b. How, practically, do you see the two of you working together as a team to accomplish these goals?

c. What will your part be on the team?

d. How do you feel about this?

If you feel negative about your role, spend time in prayer. Ask God to change your attitude or show you how to change the plan.

3. Write a letter to your husband. Tell him how, during the next year, you want to bless him. Include characteristics of a husband-lover and your role as a missionary.

4. Discuss with your husband the questions item 2 above poses. Pray through your responses.

Chapter 5

Spiritual Warfare

Each of us has entered into battle with Satan. We have joined the opposing team. Satan's goal is to tackle us and take us out of the game. For those of us in full-time Christian service, the stakes even are higher. God has called us into vocations that have kingdom purpose. Satan is strongly opposed not just to your success but also to your presence, because you are indwelt by the Holy Spirit of God. Satan detests you. As a missionary you may enter a part of the world that Satan has had under his thumb for a long time. He is not willing to give up control easily. Daily you will find yourself faced with his defensive and often offensive tactics.

One summer our family accompanied an American team to a village. We were constructing a chapel for the village's Baptist church, which had no building. The Orthodox Church, the official church of Romania, in different degrees opposed our presence. In this particular village the Orthodox priest was unusually hostile to us. On our first day of building he gathered a group of about 100 people who in force descended on us. They were ranting and raving and throwing accusations at us. Some even threw some rocks at us and at the building. They claimed, among other things, that we were there to kidnap their children and eat them. As my husband and I and a few of the translators talked to these folks, the visiting American team prayed. The leaders went together to the mayor. With his blessings the mayor allowed us to stay. But the priest and his followers didn't give up. Across the street from the chapel site they built a holy site to bless the area, since our presence and our building "defiled" their village. And the priest excommunicated the woman who lived next to the church because she let us use her land to hold our Vacation Bible School for the village children.

No mistake: this was a satanic attack. It was so blatant that it almost was humorous. I knew we had the power in this situation and knew that God would claim the victory. But Satan does not always work in such an obvious way. We know to stay away from witch doctors and voodoo, but we don't see the more subtle ways in which he gains ground in our lives. Too often we are blindsided by him, because we don't expect him to show up when and how he does. Learning how Satan works is essential to victorious resistance. For me this boils down to the four questions that introduce these next sections.

Culture shock or warfare?

After I had been in Romania for about a year, I realized a horrible fact. Almost every other missionary I knew was struggling with discouragement, doubt, all-consuming anger, and utter frustration. Several had marital problems. One friend even confessed that she no longer was certain whether she was a Christian! Conflict existed among colleagues; jealousy arose over who had the nicest house. I don't know what I expected to find on the mission field, but I didn't expect to find this sort of behavior and attitudes among the missionaries themselves. And I wasn't free from guilt either. I was surprised to find how my attitudes were focused on myself and my own comfort and not at all on God's vision for Romania.

One day as I read in Scripture about spiritual warfare, I realized what a victory Satan was having right under my own nose. This wasn't just the flesh still lifting its ugly head. It wasn't just culture shock. This was all-out warfare; we were losing. The amazing thing is that no one recognized it as such. We all were surprised. Not one of us was living in victory—experiencing the power of Christ's resurrection and witnessing the freedom from our flesh that He promises if we follow Him. And yet not one of us blamed Satan. Most of us blamed our new country and its inhabitants and called it *culture shock.*

Please understand—culture shock is a real thing. It takes some getting used to when you move to a new place. That's even true if you're just moving from Georgia to Arkansas. The changes are a little more severe if you're moving to New York and are even greater if you go to Guam or Canada. But if you go to a place in which no one speaks your language and suddenly *cald* means hot and *rece* means cold, the shock can be pretty severe. However many people mistake for culture shock Satan's stampede into our lives, so they don't fight when they should. Our senses are bombarded with brand-new stimuli; they go into shock. But I venture to say that during this time, we get a truer glimpse into our souls than at any other time, because we haven't had time to condition ourselves to the sin and ugliness around us. We haven't programmed in a correct response. We are left without a cheat sheet and have to wing it, so to speak. In such times the depth of our knowledge of God and His ways are put on trial. More often than not we are found guilty of not having absorbed nearly as much of His fragrance as we thought we had.

It's like a kid doing algebra. He learns the formulas first thing; then you give him 10 problems to do. He does them and makes a few mistakes. The next day, you give him the same 10 problems; he does them with fewer mistakes. The next day, you give him the same 10 problems; he has only one mistake. After a week he can do them all perfectly. They are based on the right principles, but he has memorized the problems as well. So on day eight you replace two of the problems with different ones.

He slows down a bit and has to think a little more but manages to get one right and the other one close. After another couple of days he has the two new ones under his belt. Then one day you give him a whole new set of problems—all at once, all brand-new. He knows the principles, but he's never used them on these problems. He misses almost every one. His knowledge is not as great as it seemed. It only seemed great because he knew the problems.

As new missionaries this is what things were like for us. All the problems had changed. We knew the principles of godly living but had not ever practiced them in this context. What better time for Satan to attack us than when we are foundering around trying to figure out this new set of problems. The problem is genuine, but being unprepared for the satanic attack is dangerous, because it leaves you with your guard down. The problem begins to snowball.

What starts as a basic dislike for the way the people in your new country urinate on the sidewalk ends up as a hatred for the entire culture. What begins as a frustration that the system doesn't work in an efficient manner ends up with your being angry at the official representatives of the government with whom you have to work to get your visa. While you wait, you find yourself mumbling obscenities under your breath. What begins as a shyness from feeling uncomfortable with this new language ends with you literally hiding in your house for fear that someone may try to talk to you and when you reply, they will laugh at you. The list can go on and on.

The reaction to the new culture is normal, but unfortunately Satan's manipulation of the reaction is far too normal as well. For a time you feel useless and have no joy in your service.

Once I realized that Satan was waging war on my emotions, I was able to fight him off. The Bible tells us that he is a formidable foe, but he is not one to fear. We can know his strategies without quaking at his presence. He will fight against us. He will stay near us. Be prepared. And we are assured the victory if we will but stand our ground.

Friend or foe?

Also be aware of the means through which he may attack. I still was in language school when Satan surprise-attacked me. The dirty deed was done through another missionary. She was not with our organization but lived in the same town as we did. We were casual acquaintances but ended up together on a tour of the northeastern part of Romania. We spent very little time together on the trip. This was because I didn't care for her personality and didn't care to be around her. After we arrived home, she visited my house one day and proceeded to tell me that I was a horrible mother and wife. She pointed out all my faults in these areas as well as weaknesses in my character in general and in my abilities as a missionary. She was a virtual stranger! In my lifetime I maybe had spent a total of two hours with her, yet she unfairly passed judgment on me.

Although I was stunned beyond belief and definitely could see that something wasn't right, her words still stung. The attack was timed perfectly. I had been on the mission field for only six months and was smack-dab in the middle of dealing with culture shock and the self-esteem issues that accompanied the new territory.

During this time I didn't feel competent at much of anything. I couldn't speak intelligently, couldn't minister effectively, couldn't figure out how to love a people and culture that were so different from ours, didn't know how to partner with my husband, and had yet to figure out how to be a good mom, by my definition, in a culture that didn't seem to have many options for kids with free time on their hands. But still I hated thinking that I could make such a bad impression on anyone, however incorrect it might be.

God was so gracious to me during that time. During the actual event He gave me a calmness that was unnatural. Afterward He gave me the presence of mind to verify the accurateness of her statements instead of just believing them. God showed me that she was way off-base. He undergirded me and even allowed me to reach out to her in love and forgiveness. He helped me recognize as spiritual warfare her behavior. But my first question to Him was "Could a missionary be used as a tool of Satan?" The answer was a resounding "YES!" I was shocked but was sure that it was true.

This not only opened my eyes to the possibility of Satan using another believer to deceive me, it also served as a warning that He may try to use me as an instrument of destruction in another's life. I became more aware of my actions and of what I said when I was with colleagues and nationals. When we got together, we had a huge temptation to share our woes and hardships. Some of this was a healthy processing of our emotions, but sometimes it amounted to culture-bashing or even to God-bashing. When we were with nationals, we had to be careful not to criticize their ways and their customs in the name of God, when in reality we just hadn't adapted yet.

Do you have a friend or sister with whom you can share everything? Then you are blessed, but be sure that your conversations don't turn into gossip or gripe sessions. Do you have the gift of prophecy or teaching? Wonderful, but don't let Satan tempt you to get in the flesh and use your gifts for his purposes. I'm sure the woman I mentioned thought that she was exhorting me in the name of Christ, but her observations were blurred, her words were harsh, and Satan misused her gift of being outspoken. If she really had loved me, then she would have held her tongue and prayed diligently for me. After this woman finished her discourse on my failures, she asked me, "Can't you take constructive criticism from a friend?" I responded to her, "Yes, but this isn't constructive. You aren't yet my friend."

I want to be an aroma of Christ and not the stench of Satan.

Down-time or losing the battle?

We all need down-time. We need to unwind and relax and not think for a while. But how we relax and unwind is of utmost importance. The world is great at giving us ways to unwind and making them all sound very legitimate—even merited. But the world is Satan's domain. Keep your guard up even when you are at rest. Maybe you like television or movies or great restaurants or family outings or game nights or shopping. In and of itself, whatever you like probably isn't bad, but when it becomes the foundation of your joy, then you have a problem.

As a missionary overseas this especially is noticeable, because in many countries entertainment and relaxation activities simply are not a part of the nationals' lives. They don't have the money or the time to put much effort into having fun. The lack of such things and people's preoccupation with them makes your dependence on them stand out even more. As the new culture gets to you, you feel a need to escape for a little while. You begin to search for something that brings comfort—a shopping trip to buy a new shirt, an American meal at McDonald's, a rented movie from a video store. In small doses this can be healthy, but if you start living for the times of escape, you have a problem.

A friend once wrote to say that for some time she had struggled over a soap opera. She knew that watching it day after day wasn't good for her, but she was hooked; it was affecting her life. She finally gained the victory. This was my response to her:

Thanks for your note. It is really encouraging to hear how God is at work in your life. I'm glad you had victory over the soap opera. That is a big battle. The TV can be used for good but I think it is such a tool of Satan to the general populace. It is such a trap. I have struggled with it too, and often threaten to get rid of it altogether, but never have gone through with it. My latest battle was with "Friends," a show that started coming on here. I had seen it a couple of times in the States and thought it was pretty trashy, though extremely funny. It came on here every night at 10:30. During the summer it got dark around 10 and at 10:30, I was feeding Andrew and the kids were upstairs with their daddy. I got into a habit of watching it every night, excusing the fact that almost every episode was centered around sex and they habitually accepted and made light of things that God hates, because it was so funny and their humor made me laugh. Well, they took it off and I was crushed. Though I'd been rationalizing it for weeks before and felt I should be spending my time better, I was really sad when it was gone. Actually I was downright depressed when I didn't have that to look forward to at the end of the day. Silly, I know. But it has been so great to have that out of my life. My prayer life has been better, I am a better mom because I am more involved in bedtime since I'm not trying to watch that silly show, etc. I am glad God saw fit to remove it when He did. In His mercy he took away my choice. I only wish I would have made the choice myself.

The television show had become a trap. I was using it for my down-time. For just a few minutes I could forget that I was in another country far away from home. I watched Americans who had a humor that I could understand and appreciate. I laughed at it. I found comfort in it. But it wasn't of the Lord. It was not a positive influence on me. It became a problem for me.

I wasn't planning for Satan to attack me through such a little thing; I wasn't prepared. Thankfully God rescued me. Since then I have tried to be wiser. Be aware of the little ways in which Satan will try to distract you from having the mind of Christ.

Discouraged or under his heel?

The last way I'll mention that Satan often attacks the unaware is through disappointments and discouragement. We want so badly to see God use us—to see Him at work around us. When we don't, we begin to feel abandoned and alone. But this is a misunderstanding.

God always is at work in the hearts and through the prayers of His people. Only sometimes we don't see it—we're not tuned in. Satan wants to keep us perpetually distracted so that we live in this state of discouragement.

Some weeks I have great times with the Lord—quiet times with few interruptions, prayer times that really seem to reach to heaven. During those weeks I am amazed at what God is doing in me, through me, sometimes to me. Then during some weeks my quiet time is when I'm asleep; prayers are breathed while I'm on my way to my next event. Unfailingly during these times I wonder where God is and why He is not pleased to bring forth fruit around me.

Have you ever noticed the time God gives us to reflect on Him? He provides the time to get our perspective right. He invites us to approach His throne and to see things as He sees them. He knows that we need that time to quiet our souls. He always provides, if we just take advantage of it. For me it is that few minutes after my day has ended and the kids are asleep—I need to unwind—do I do it before the Lord, or before the TV? When I wake up a few minutes before the alarm clock goes off, do I accept that as a gift from the Lord and rise to meet with Him, or do I roll over and go back to sleep? When the kids all go outside and a rare quietness reigns in the house, do I start cleaning up their tracks on the floor, or, since my time in the Word was cut short that morning, do I take those few minutes to finish it? I have begun to notice how I spent my few extra minutes. Sometimes I am ashamed that this lack of self-discipline makes me an easy target for Satan.

We don't get discouraged because God fails to act. We get discouraged because we allow Satan to distract us from seeing what God is doing. Our spiritual sight becomes dull if we are not honing it consistently in the Word and in prayer and we begin to look only at the surface. Scripture constantly reminds us to dwell on things above—to have the mind of Christ, to think on the pure and lovely. God knows our tendency to get distracted from what really is important. If Satan can distract us with the things of this world, then we are incapable of seeing the eternal things going on around us.

The normal Christian life

Satan is a powerful agent. Knowing this is important so that you will be prepared to fight Him in kind. But knowing and understanding the limitations of his power and how he works around them is just as important. He can't keep us doomed to hell. The power of salvation is greater than is his power. If God chooses to save you, then Satan can do nothing about it. But if you allow it, he can make your walk with Christ dull and monotonous—without freedom, without power. He can convince us that the Christian life doesn't have much to it. He can cheat us out of the joy that is ours by inheritance.

Often when at a young age we accept Christ, we put Christianity in a box and forget that it is an awesome, life-changing, heaven-and-earth-moving power that has filled us. We see it as a rulebook to live by—the "don'ts" that will keep us pure and safe. Jesus rarely, if ever, spoke about what He didn't want us to do; yet that often is how we summarize the Christian life. I don't do that because I'm a Christian. But what DO you DO because you're a Christian? How does Christ manifest Himself in your life? Jesus' indwelling presence is not there merely to help you abstain from worldly pleasures; it is there to imbue you with the strength to do all that He has called you to do and to do it in a phenomenal way. What has He called you to do? Are you doing it? Are you doing it well? Is your Christian life an ever-changing, ever-growing relationship that evolves daily with your maturity and understanding of God's will in your life? Or is it a past experience that is the basis merely for your mode of living and the degree of dissatisfaction that you have with yourself?

When Jesus spoke of a life of following Him, it was a life of freedom and power and hope. We tend to be content with so little—to become complacent and not reach higher for something that is better, to live with a sense of disappointment that our lives aren't much more and to think that this is the norm.

If you're wondering whether this describes you, then ask yourself the following questions. Are you filled with joy? Are you overflowing with hope? Do you see the power of God working in you and through you? Or are you constantly filled with regrets that you are not living your life the way you wish you were—that you are not being the mom, wife, person that you thought you would be? Are you plagued with doubts that your life is making a difference in this world?

When Peter understood and confessed who Jesus was, "*the Christ, the Son of the Living God*", Jesus proclaimed (Matt. 16:16-19) that His church would be built on this truth. Of its strength and power He said, "*the gates of Hades shall not over-power it.*" And to Peter He said, "*I will give you the keys of the kingdom of heaven; and whatever you shall bind on earth shall be bound in heaven and whatever you shall loose on earth shall be loosed in heaven.*" This is the power—the living, pulsating, vibrant power that has saved you and me from death. Peter understood this spiritual truth only because God revealed it to him. If you are not living the Christian life with the zeal and power that this truth brings to it, then ask God to reveal it to you anew. Maybe Satan is winning the battle and you don't even realize it. Maybe he has lulled you into a state of complacency. If this is not the case, then rest assured that sooner or later he will try this tactic on you. Regularly examine your passion for God and your vision for following Him. Be aware that the enemy wants to quell both.

Be prepared

If you leave for the mission field and expect to meet up with Satan only on rare, mystical occasions, you will not be prepared for the real battle. The battle over your soul may be won, but the battle for the state of your soul while you are on this earth is of utmost importance to him. He wants to render you useless and miserable. Spend time in God's Word so that you will be able to recognize when Satan is lying to you, deceiving you, discourag-ing you, and accusing you. Only with a deep, heart understanding of truth will you be able to put forth a worthy defense and have victory.

QUESTIONS FOR DISCUSSION

1. Talk about the four sometimes-surprising ways that Satan attacks us as missionaries. Do you have personal examples?

2. Discuss how we can be prepared for ways that Satan might attack us.

3. Discuss how Satan has been active in your life as you have prepared for missionary service. How have you overcome?

4. Look up and read together the following verses: Ephesians 6:12-13, James 4:7, Romans 12:1-2.

5. Spend time in prayer and include the following:

• submit yourself to God and to His plans for you
• recognize that this is resisting Satan's plans and desires for you
• acknowledge that Satan now must flee from you. Thank God for this.

Chapter 6

Worship

Nothing is more important or more at risk in the life of a missionary than is worship time with God—whether corporately or privately. Worshiping effectively and meaningfully in a second culture takes creativity. It also takes patience. Knowing ahead of time what worship is and what it isn't is important.

Worship isn't Sunday-morning church

When I first arrived on the mission field, I looked forward to worshiping with national believers. I just knew that it would be an awe-inspiring time of broadening my understanding of true worship. But after I returned home from church, I was very deflated. I had not enjoyed the worship service at all! I'm sure that God was there, but He did not show Himself to us in the traditional ways I was used to seeing Him. Somehow I missed out altogether. Between juggling kids, trying to keep my feet warm, not understanding a word that was said, and trying to keep the scarf from falling off my head, no wonder that no awe was forthcoming! But instead of recognizing the situation for what it was, we continued to depend on that Sunday service to be our time of worship. The result was that we began to dry up spiritually.

About six months after we arrived, we had a meeting with missionaries from other countries in our region. The first time we began to sing in English and be exhorted from the Word in English, I sat and wept. I was hungry for some food. I was hungry for worship. I realized then that I was far too dependent on others for my worship experience. If I was to survive, I couldn't go six months to a year between worship times. I was going to have to learn to worship on my own.

I'm not encouraging you to abandon national services. In the life of a missionary they are a necessity. Worship with the people you are there to serve. In time these services will become enjoyable. But during the interim, do not forfeit true worship of God. Attend the services, meet the people, learn the language, and understand the culture, but don't depend on those two hours every week to fulfill your need to worship God.

Worship is possible without a crowd

I really didn't think I could worship without the help of "church." I knew I needed to, but the thought of getting into worship alone seemed strange. I needed the choir to help set the mood and the pastor to tell me when to reflect and pray and the sermon to enrich my life. At least that's what I thought. In theory I knew that worship could be personal between me and God, but I felt the absence of the ceremony. I still love that today, but I have learned how to worship on my own. Truly I have benefited greatly to be in a place in which I don't need the extras. Worship is very personal now; to have it I don't have to depend on the time or place or people.

We also have learned to worship as a family. One of the things I missed most about America was the children's programs at church. These made church fun for the kids; my children always looked forward to attending. In Romania that wasn't the case. Very little church programming is aimed at children; what existed usually was more rigid than my kids enjoyed. Every Sunday they actually dreaded church. Soon this deficit became a blessing, because we started taking a more active role in teaching our kids. They love our family worship time; we are teaching them what true worship is. When we returned to the States on home assignment, I resented the intrusion into our family the myriad of programs caused. We never worshiped together. I felt as though the church was splitting us apart. I eventually began to enjoy the freedom and in doing so felt less personal responsibility for what my kids were learning. I began to appreciate the circumstances that had forced me to do what I never would have done on my own.

As good as personal worship can be, supplementing your worship times also is important, because some of the elements of group worship can't be done alone. One such element is teaching from the Word. Study the Word on your own. God has given us His Holy Spirit to teach us. If necessary we could live only with a Bible and our own minds and never stop learning. But necessity aside, God desires to bless us through other men and women of God. Second Corinthians 1:3-4 says, *Blessed be the God and Father of our Lord Jesus Christ, the Father of mercies and God of all comfort; who comforts us in all our affliction so that we will be able to comfort those who are in any affliction with the comfort with which we ourselves are comforted by God.* He expects us to learn from each other. The Internet is a tremendous resource for print and audio sermons and links to live worship services. Some churches enjoy sending tapes or CD's of recent sermons. This is a blessing. Until you are proficient in the language, listening to sermons in a different language will not become edifying to you. Even when you begin to understand the sermon, you will have a tendency to evaluate it instead of learn from it.

But don't go for years without hearing a good sermon. Continue being exhorted and challenged by a Bible teacher. This will make you a better missionary and keep you sharp spiritually.

Another supplement is fellowship. I didn't realize how much of the fun of going to church was seeing my friends there and communicating with them on a meaningful level. In a second culture that type of relationship sometimes is slow to develop even at church. You need fellowship. If missionaries in your city aren't doing something to meet this need, then just pick one or two other families and meet regularly with them to pray, talk, cry, sing, and worship. This will help keep you accountable and will make you stronger individually and as a group. We and another family regularly shared a family worship time. This helped us to worship with our children and made worship fun for them, too. Our group consisted of just a few people, but we had church.

Another good supplement is Christian music from home. As much as you may love the music of your new home, singing along with the lyrics or hearing a familiar hymn is irreplaceable. Music touches our souls like no other artistic expression does. God intended it to be used for His glory. I keep a tape player in the kitchen, since that is the place in which I spend most of my time. When I am in the midst of the witching hour (you know—the one right before supper when everybody—including you—is hungry and tired), nothing helps me to get my focus back on the pure and lovely things of God as much as does a good song. Before I know it, I'm singing along with it and reflecting on the goodness of God.

The point of worship is for you to commune with God. It was not until "church" as I knew it was taken away and I learned how to worship on my own that I realized that often I actually wasn't worshiping in church. We go through the ceremony but don't really stand in the presence of God and enjoy Him. Even after church in my second culture became more enjoyable, I had to be careful truly to worship and not just go through the motions.

Worship is a weapon in spiritual warfare

Our main weapon in spiritual warfare is maintaining our fellowship with God, our Father. Through alone time in His Word, in conversation with Him, and through the encouragement and fellowship of other believers, truth is revealed and understood, our enemy's plans are uncovered, and our minds are made sharp and wise. Without it we are as good as defeated.

James 4:7 gives us the recipe for victory in spiritual warfare: *Submit therefore to God. Resist the devil and he will flee from you.* It sounds really simple and it is, but it also often is misunderstood. We mistakenly read these as two commands that have no relationship to each other. First we submit; then we resist. But submitting to God and resisting the devil are simultaneous actions. Resisting Satan is impossible without submitting ourselves to God; the very act of submitting ourselves to God is resisting the god of this world who reigns through our flesh.

When we are saved, we give our lives over to God and submit completely to Him. But often through the course of our lives a little at a time we take back control. Through these fragments Satan is given power in our lives. If we totally are submitted to God, Satan has no place to get a foothold. But when we take back that control in an area of our lives, we seem to create a ledge on which Satan can balance. Sometimes this happens so gradually that we are not even aware that we have re-claimed an area of our life. That is where worship enters the picture. Through our time in God's presence He is able to point out these areas of sin so that we can be pure before Him and safe from the attacks of the enemy.

Suppose a young woman struggles in the area of singleness. When she gave her life to God, this was not a problem—she gladly surrendered control of all areas of her life and trusted God to do His perfect will in her life. But as time goes on, she becomes discontent with her state and dissatisfied with God's will for her in this area. This becomes the ledge on which Satan perches; from there has had ample opportunity to torment her. She loses her joy, her vision, and her intimacy with God. She no longer takes the time to worship Him, be with Him, and learn from Him. She becomes blind to her own sin. She decides to take matters into her own hands and dates many men. She tries to find security and love through sex and physical intimacy. She isn't satisfied with the farce of a Christian life she has and decides that religion isn't all it is cracked up to be. She blames God for the state she is in because He did not give her what she wanted. She is headed down the road to destruction. The spiritual battle for her life is raging. To win the battle over Satan she has to go back to the point of departure and give back the control of this area of her life and submit to His will for her—even if it means being single forever. Through doing this she resists what Satan wants to do in her life. She resists his plan by submitting to God's. She removes the ledge on which Satan's foot was resting. Satan has no power in the face of a believer who practices true worship.

You may be thinking that worship had nothing to do with victory; submission made the difference. But let's look at another definition of worship. Romans 12:1 says, *"I urge you therefore, brethren by the mercies of God, to present your bodies a living and holy sacrifice, acceptable to God, which is your spiritual service of worship."* When we present ourselves to God, we offer ourselves to Him, accept His headship over us, and submit to His will. This clearly is involved in worship. Our act of worship involves recognizing Who God is, acknowledging the rights He has over our lives, and agreeing with Him on His plan for us. This and only this gives God the honor He deserves. From these foundational elements of worship the praise and adoration and thanksgiving that we normally associate with worship arises.

A better example may be one that hits closer to home. When I was writing the chapter on spiritual warfare, I was unaware that Satan was so close by. I was talking to a friend about the fact that I really had been depressed for the last couple of days. I wasn't excited about anything in my life; I wasn't content; I felt anxious. She pointed out that this sounded as though it were spiritual warfare. Then the light shone. I realized indeed that Satan was very opposed to what I was writing and was trying to distract me. I had not sinned or taken back control of anything, but the solution was the same. I had to go to God and submit to Him. I had to read the Word and get my perspective right and choose to believe the truth of what God says over the lies that Satan was telling me. I couldn't make the feelings change, but I couldn't give into them either. I had to choose to submit to what God tells me is true over what Satan was telling me was true. I felt hopeless, but God says that through Jesus we always have hope; I felt anxious, but God tells me that no need exists ever to be anxious, because He will provide all that I need if I focus on Him; I felt discontented, but God tells me that I can rest in Him. Only through time and dwelling on the truth was I able to choose to live by what I knew to be true instead of by what my emotions were telling me. This was submission to God; this was resisting the devil. He had no choice but to flee.

Worship isn't the same as ministry

Many times those of us in full-time ministry mistake our ministry time with our worship time. This is especially true if you are a Bible teacher. Although preparing for a lesson or a presentation can be a catalyst for a true worship time, it is not always inherently so. Studying often is objective and distant. Worship always is personal and up-close.

We can get so caught up in the doing that we forget to stop and reflect on both our lives and on God. Because of my being a missionary, I often find myself involved in some sort of position in which the Word is being taught in the presence of non-believers. Instead of listening to the words and applying them to myself, I catch myself thinking about to whom this particular point might apply and hoping that the person is listening to what the preacher is saying. Nothing is wrong with that, but I benefit from getting out of teacher-evangelist mode sometimes and apply the truths to myself.

In the Mary-and-Martha syndrome, Martha was so busy doing the work that she not only didn't worship Jesus, but she rebuked Him. She got so focused on her needs that she thought that Jesus needed to be doing her bidding. We may say that is absurd, but don't we do the same thing? We run off on a tangent and then ask God to bless us. We feel abandoned by Him if He doesn't. Our works are in vain if they indeed are our works and not His works. The only safeguard we have against this happening is participating in true worship.

Jesus, our example

Jesus is our best example of worship. He was God Himself, yet He found Himself needing to spend time with the Father to accomplish all the things He was sent to earth to do. In this area we can learn from Him.

At nearly every major event in His life, He prayed and fellowshiped with God. He did this at His baptism, the transfiguration, His arrest, and on the cross. But the one that I like the best is before He chose His disciples. He spent a night in prayer before He announced His selection. Even though He was God, He conferred with the Father before this event. What a beautiful picture of submission and intimacy! He and God were working together to accomplish redemption for the people God loved. He had to stay in constant contact with the Father.

Have you ever noticed how intentional Jesus was in His daily walk—not only on the large scale of heading toward Jerusalem and the crucifixion but even on the smaller scale of what He did each day? And yet as deliberate as He was, He also was patient and accommodating when His plans got interrupted. I believe this also is because He always was conversing with God about what He was to do and knew the plan for His life and for each day of it. Nothing took Him by surprise, nothing scared Him, and nothing flustered Him, because He knew that God the Father was orchestrating the entire thing.

Luke 5:1 says that the multitude was pressing in around Him. He would leave the people; they would follow. But never did He get angry or tell them to go away. In chapter 9 this happened. Let's look at how Jesus reacted to this intrusion. *When the apostles returned, they gave an account to Him of all that they had done. Taking them with Him, He withdrew by Himself to a city called Bethsaida. But the crowds were aware of this and followed Him; and welcoming them, He began speaking to them about the kingdom of God and curing those who had need of healing* (10-11).

Don't you love how Jesus welcomed them? He had hoped to be alone, but He was gracious when they encroached on His privacy. He didn't even just politely tell them to go away. He taught them and healed them and met their needs. He purposely had left the crowds, because He intended to be alone with His closest friends.

Yet when those plans were interrupted, He responded graciously. He understood that God was the master of His time and was sovereign in the way it was used. He rested in that knowledge. He was God's instrument and not there to meet His own needs. How different from our thinking—that our time is our own and that we have a right to our privacy.

This knowledge that God was orchestrating the events of His time on earth also kept Him from fearing people or the possibility that things would not go as expected. Luke 13:31-33 says, *Just at that time some Pharisees came up, saying to Him, "Go away, leave here, for Herod wants to kill you." And He said to them, "Go and tell that fox, 'Behold, I cast out demons and perform cures today and tomorrow, and the third day I reach My goal. Nevertheless I must journey on today and tomorrow and the next day; for it cannot be that a prophet would perish outside of Jerusalem."* Jesus knew that God, not Herod, was the master controller. Herod could do nothing outside of God's intended plan. He trusted God the Father completely. I believe that these two characteristics of Jesus' life are connected. If we know that God is in control of our days, then we can accept the interruptions as God-appointed.

Certainly we can say that Jesus' insight and accommodating nature sprang from the fact that He was God-man. But as much as He fully was God, He fully was human. We are told that He experienced every temptation that we experience. Therefore I believe that He was tempted to be anxious about His time, how it was spent, and if all would go according to the plan. I believe that Jesus was able to be as He was, in the flesh, because of His understanding of His need and dependence on God the Father.

The Bible tells us that Jesus often got up early or went off by Himself to pray. Only twice are we privy to what He said during those times—the high-priestly prayer and at Gethsemane. Both show us that during this time of worship, He submitted himself to God the Father in obedience and trust. At Gethsemane He was completely given over to God and put His Father's will above His own. In the high-priestly prayer, He acknowledged the fact that all that He had done, He had done at the Father's command and to please the Father. Through these prayers He reveals His submissive and humble spirit. The fact that He sought out these times with the Father, made time to interact with Him in a personal way, and honored Him through total submission to His will shows us the importance of worship as well as the result of such intimacy with God.

If Jesus saw the need to worship the Father while He walked on this earth, how much more do we need the same?

QUESTIONS FOR DISCUSSION

1. What do you know about "worship" with other believers in your country of service? How does it differ from the type of worship to which you're accustomed?

2. List some of the main elements of worship found in these Scriptures: Romans 12:1,2; Psalm 95:6; John 4:24; Psalm 105:2; Hebrews 13:15.

3. How can you make sure that in your new culture you will continue to worship on a regular basis?

4. Why is worshiping important?

5. Spend time in prayer as you commit to God your desire to worship and learn of Him.

Chapter 7

Parenting

Our first exposure to Romania was in 1991, when we were involved in a volunteer mission trip. Most of the other folks on the team went into the villages. We were asked to stay in Bucharest. Not a coincidence, I'm sure. During that trip God and I were at odds the whole time. I sensed that He was revealing to me that we would return to Romania; I didn't want ever to be there again. I stood in the apartment where we were staying and looked out the window at the scene below. A bare piece of land that was mostly mud was the home of a rusty swingset frame with one metal swing; several mangy, undernourished street dogs; a couple of small, dirty cars up on their sides (the position Romanians use to do repairs), and a metal bar used for hanging and beating rugs. Next to this were a small parking lot with a handful of dingy looking cars that were painted with flat dull colors and several small, metal-roofed, concrete buildings that seemed to be garages of some sort. Like the buildings that surrounded them they were drab and ugly. Several dumpsters contained overflowing garbage. A myriad of windows—hundreds—looked down on the same, despairing scene. I didn't like what I saw. But I didn't worry for myself. I had an 8-month-old baby—a precious boy—and I wanted only the best for him. I couldn't imagine choosing the scene before me as his playground. I made it clear to God that I was not happy with His plan.

As parents, when our children are concerned, we have a protective-instinct nature. We want the best for them. We don't want anything to stand between them and happiness. Sometimes we are so focused on this happiness that we forget what actually brings it about. Didn't we find our own peace and joy only when we met Jesus and surrendered our lives to Him? Neither our surroundings nor any material possessions brought lasting joy. Weren't we gladly willing to give up all the comforts of home when we committed ourselves to mission service, because we knew that the comforts really didn't matter anyway in comparison to knowing and following the Master? And yet when we gave birth to our own child, we immediately desired to give him the best that this world has to offer. Suddenly those things that we abandoned seem much more important.

When God calls us to follow Him into a place that looks less than ideal, we are faced with this double standard and are forced to wrestle with the issue of what, exactly, we want to pass on to our children.

During my struggle with this issue I began to understand that when God called Preston and me, He called our children, too. Since the day we married, we had been praying for them. We knew that we wanted them to be followers of Jesus. As much as doing so went against our grain some of the time, we chose to make "things" secondary in their lives and obedience primary. Although we sometimes didn't feel it, we believed that in His hands was the safest and most beneficial place that they could be, regardless of the physical surroundings. So we packed up and moved to Romania, even though all of my "mommy" instincts told me not to do so. It was the right decision; over and over God has proved it to us.

We now have four children who are well-adjusted and flexible. They are growing up—not in a perfect environment but in one that centers on God's will and His provision for us. Together we watch for God to meet our needs; together we grow and change to become more like Jesus.

Keep your kids on the team—involve family in ministry

One of the great things about being a missionary family is that the work can involve all of you. Among American Christians the mom and dad work and try to leave that work at the office so they can return home and focus on the family. The relationship between parents and children often is one-dimensional. Though it could and might be otherwise, most jobs don't lend themselves to such an outcome. Mission work includes a necessity for the family to function as a unit and for the kids to feel as though they are a part of the work, because they definitely are. They often are the ones through which God works to break down walls, foster friendships, and build bridges to the community. This results in relationships that are multi-dimensional; it gives all involved a sense of being a team. When, for the first time, we went on our Stateside assignment, my kids were proud to tell everyone that they themselves, not just their parents, were missionaries. The call of God is on their lives, too. They play an important part in what we accomplish in our new country. This truth gives them a great sense of belonging and importance as well as introducing to them at a young age the concept that God desires to and does use them. As our children have grown older, we find that they love to share and tell stories of their lives as missionaries. My three oldest children all have been active in telling their classmates about Jesus; two of them actually have been involved in someone's conversion. All of them—even our 6-year-old—actively pray for their lost friends and try to be an example to them.

Of course children aren't going to preach in the churches and teach at the seminaries. Sometimes you have to be creative to involve them in what you are doing. I got involved with an orphanage for street children and went several times on day-trips to village to visit the mother and siblings of one particular child. Whenever possible I let the kids go with me, because I want them to see what our work is about and to feel a part of helping other people. We gave this family some of our toys and clothes; they made friends with the street kid who was going with us to visit his mom. And they got to see how fortunate we are.

As the kids have gotten older, we have allowed them to join in with volunteer teams to build churches, prayerwalk, or help out in other ways. Some kids even work as translators!

One of the most rewarding times occurred when a neighbor who was very upset visited me. Our family was leaving for church, but I stayed home to talk to her. Preston and the kids prayed for her as they traveled to church. Before she left the house, she professed faith in Christ. That afternoon some neighborhood kids were outside playing ball. David, our 9-year-old, went out to play with them. A few minutes later he reported to me that he had been telling one of the kids outside about Jesus and wanted a Bible to give to him. I could see that he not only was learning the importance of sharing his faith, but he was sharing the responsibility of telling our neighbors about Christ.

But along with the victories, we had to learn to deal with defeat as well. Several months later the same neighbor mentioned above stole some money from us. We had become good friends, I thought, and all of us rejoiced in her newfound faith. To my kids she was a picture of a changed life. When we realized that she had stolen money not once but several times while she was in our home, we were pretty disappointed. This led to a lot of good discussions with the kids about faith and actions and sin and forgiveness.

Before I was willing to admit that she was guilty, I was talking to David about it one day. He said, "Mom, I know you hate to admit it, and I do, too, but you have to accept that she is the one who did this." He was consoling me and was being a great team member.

When you head to the mission field, don't try to shield your kids just because things are different or difficult. Don't fear for them when the challenges of living in another culture arise. God is preparing them just as He is preparing you. They will learn of Him if you will allow it. It may mean some tears and some anger, but God will see them through the tough times. Be honest. Cry with them, doubt with them, believe with them, question with them, fear with them. You don't always have to have all the answers. But look with them to the One who does. Your relationship with your kids will be stronger and their relationships with the heavenly Father will be stronger as well. Let them be a part of what you are doing. You know that your team will have the ultimate victory, so it really can't lose.

Lead by example—your kids are watching!

Every team has a captain. In your team the captains are you and your spouse. When I was at orientation before going to the field, I was overwhelmed by all the talk of culture shock. The next two years sounded as though we were going to live in a loony-bin. My children were 2 and 4; I wondered how living with parents who were experiencing temporary insanity was going to affect them. Two years represented a pretty major chunk of their lives, especially when child psychologists are saying that a significant part of a child's personality is formed when he or she is between the ages of 3 and 6. I was, in effect, going to warp my children. At the orientation center I asked a counselor about this; he nonchalantly said, "Don't worry! As long as you are emotionally stable, they will be fine." For the past seven weeks they had been telling me that I wasn't going to BE emotionally stable; now I'm told that my kids' normalcy will depend on whether I am. Thanks a lot, counselor. That helps!

Well, the results aren't in yet on whether the warping was complete, but I did learn that, more than I realized, kids mirror their parents' attitudes and opinions. When we first arrived in language school, we were pretty taken aback by some of the cultural trends. Being the vocal person that I am, I didn't hesitate to share my opinions with whoever would listen, including my kids. Of course I was correct, so I wasn't harming them, right?

One such area was with the difference in how children are perceived and what is expected of them. In a toy store the kids would begin to try out the toys—a pretty normal thing in the States, but in Romania that was taboo. NOBODY touched the merchandise, even if it was sitting on the sidewalk begging for a child to notice it. At a park the kids weren't allowed to step on the grass. On a walk, the kids were not allowed to cut loose and act crazy. In church, which had no children's program, the kids weren't allowed to have coloring books or other quiet toys. Out of sheer frustration, we often would talk about how silly their rules were. We would tell the kids not to worry about what others thought and just do what they knew was okay to do.

But the longer we lived in that country, the less fun it was to fight the system. The best and wisest approach seemed to be just to give in and do it that country's way. We started to understand and respect how people in that country felt about some things; we became willing merely to accept others. Just as a certain code of behavior is acceptable in America, your new country has one, too. Neither code is inherently correct, but we choose to abide by it because it is part of our culture. Now we had taken on a new culture. If we were to focus on the important issues at stake, we needed to accept its codes as our own. Preston and I sometimes chose to make this change and sometimes found ourselves unconsciously making it. But our children weren't able to do so as easily or naturally.

When we were in the mall one day, I realized this (Yes! Bucharest has a mall!). The rule is that even though the mall had a fascinating water fountain with a sitting ledge around it, no one is allowed to sit or in any way approach this great temptation. I still think it is a silly rule, but nonetheless, it a rule. As I warned my kids away, because of the presence of the security guard, my son looked irritatingly at the man and said, "What a dumb rule, right, Mom?" I suddenly realized that I had fostered in my child a rebellious attitude toward authority and a disdain toward the protectors of that authority. They were getting to where they thought it was okay to break the rules if they didn't like them. Oops!

As a missionary you live in a fishbowl. This not only is true with the neighbors but with your kids, too. They are watching you and get their cues from you. Everything is new and different. They need a plumb line to know whether something is right. If you enjoy what you are doing, chances are the kids will enjoy it, too. If you are critical of the culture and the people, the kids will be, too. If you are mad at God for putting you in such a place, your kids will pick up that attitude, too.

When we were in language school, our two young children saw in us all the struggles that we experienced. They felt the tension that we felt as we tried to fit into another culture and often rejected its values. Consequently learning the language and making friends were not as easy for them as we thought it would be. They were wary, as they sensed we were. By the time our third child, Jessica, was born, we had adjusted to the culture and the people. Not surprisingly she learned the language better than the other two ever had and made friends easily with our neighbors. In later years the older two did fine, but as preschoolers their perceptions of things mirrored our own. The result was adaptation at a slower pace.

I have seen this same trend in other families. Those families that accept and embrace the culture have children who have done the same. Those parents that are critical and negative toward all of the changes have children who are the same. I am not saying this to scare you, but be aware of the impact you will have on your children. They feel what you feel, parrot what you say, and perceive what you perceive. Of course sometimes the actions of your children have little if anything to do with you. They are individuals with their own spiritual struggles, especially as they age. The good news is that God is big enough to take care of them, just as He takes care of you.

I now know what the counselor at orientation was trying to say. These are not words that are comforting to hear. We want to hear that regardless of our own sinful and fleshly behavior, our children will be preserved by God in sainthood. Well, it just ain't so! The hard, cold facts are that you are intimately connected with your children. What you do and feel affects them in a big way. But don't let this scare you. Just as you will survive the first two years, so will your children. Just as you will learn and grow and change, so will they. Just as God is sufficient for you in all things, He is sufficient for them. Let the knowledge that they are watching spur you to keep a guard on your hearts and mouths, but also let it encourage you to be transparent with them as you learn the lessons that God has for you to learn. Don't be ashamed of the fact that you struggle. The way you deal with the struggle will teach your children priceless lessons.

Temptation to change parenting styles/new expectations

One of the most shocking things that occurred when we crossed the Atlantic was that I suddenly wasn't viewed as a perfect mother. This new culture had new expectations for me and for my children. As I battled with finding my niche, I was rather disheartened to see that these nationals didn't perceive I was good at the one area in which I thought I excelled. Their rules were different; they thought my ways were strange.

The most obvious of these differences was the way I dressed my children. For nine months of the year Romanian children wear layered clothing (and a wool hat, to boot). Romanians generally don't have good heating and don't have access to medicines that we do. All their energies are geared at protecting their children from illness. Babies are bundled up so tightly that all you can see is their eyes. They aren't allowed to crawl or play on the floor, because the floor is cold. They may get in a draft. For the same reasons their ears must be covered. They never allow their children to go barefoot, because the sidewalks are filthy and the grass near the sidewalks has been "used" by the dogs (and the street children). In the summer younger girls generally don't wear swimsuits that cover their chest, because the Romanians fear that the wetness against the chest cavity is dangerous (the older ones don't do it for other reasons, I suppose). The list goes on and on. On a daily basis I was stopped on the street and was criticized for the way I dressed my child. Even when I tried to do it their way, it was inadequate. They often wear four or five layers of shirts in the winter! I never even thought to do that. After about four to five years, I began to understand the reasoning behind what they did. Some of the habits were based on a lack of medical knowledge, but many of them sprang from years of living in a poor country with a very low standard of living and no access to good medical care. It was survival.

As a missionary you are to be a student of the culture and learn from the people. That is the only way you can earn their respect and convince them that you have their best interests at heart. This is how you earn a right to be heard. So how do you draw the line between learning and forsaking what you know to be true? You and I know that a drafty room isn't going to cause pneumonia, so do we keep all the windows closed even on a hot day? Do we keep our babies off the floor for the sake of appearances when we know that crawling is a good developmental stage in a baby's life? As you embark on your life as a missionary, you will have to deal with questions such as these and many others. No pat answers exists—just a few guidelines.

• Never say, "It's my right to do such and such." As a follower of Christ, you have given up all your rights.

• Never say, "I don't really care what they think." Paul tells us to be accommodating of another's convictions within the body of Christ, if we aren't disobeying God to do so. If the other person is offended, let it be at the cross and not at our attitude toward their culture.

• Never go against what you know to be right. I'm not talking about opinions here but facts. For example feeding newborn infants hot tea instead of mother's milk is not nutritionally sound. You know this. Don't compromise. You may become a teacher to people who really want to know better.

• When you don't understand a cultural trend, don't assume it's stupid. Assume that others have a good reason for doing things this way; try to find out what that reason is. Remember that whatever they are doing, to them it is perfectly normal.

With these guidelines you can work out the details. Each culture will be different. Each person will deal with the situation differently. Make glorifying God your first concern. He will give wisdom when you need it.

Being different

Your child always will be different from other kids. He or she isn't the same nationality as the people you will serve. Once you've lived in a foreign country, he or she will be different from the average American kid as well. In a way your child won't fit anywhere. Whenever I've heard this said, it always sounded so negative. Actually I think this situation can be very positive. Your children will learn to think independently; they will have a much broader worldview. They will not be so easily influenced by other kids, because they've seen a lot. And because of the nature of the work they ideally have a close working relationship with you—their parents. However, feeling as though you fit somewhere is healthy. This is where the presence of other Americans enters in.

When we first moved, I thought that we would live among the Romanians and go to school with them and pretty much stay away from other Americans. But as the kids grew older, I began to see that they needed someone with whom they could share an identity. They needed to know that the experiences they were having weren't isolated and that others understood how they felt and how they thought. As beneficial as being the one who doesn't follow the crowd is, this can be tough if you never are in a crowd at all. We have learned that time with fellow missionaries is necessary, too. Yes, your children are missionaries; they, too, are called; God will take care of them. But you still need to be aware of their needs and give them a healthy emotional environment in which to grow up. They are your kids first and missionaries second.

When the time arose to choose a school for our kids, we had to face this issue. The Romanian school system had many problems that concerned us. Also it didn't really welcome foreign children. We never had known anyone successful in enrolling their children. We hoped that one private, Christian, Romanian school would be a little different from the public schools in its forms of discipline and the behavior of its teachers. Because it was not accredited and the government didn't have jurisdiction over the school, it would allow us to enroll. We decided to try for that. But by midsummer this school still didn't even know if it would hold classes because of a lack of teachers, funds, and a building. At this point we decided to look into the Christian MK school in the city. It was a good learning environment; the values to which it held were our own. We knew that the quality of education would be high. We could trust the teachers to treat our children with respect. For these reasons we decided on this school. Although it was not what we originally wanted, ultimately we had to choose what was best for the kids. We didn't want them to live in an American sub-culture, but neither did we want them to grow up with a hatred for school and no love of learning. We had to put their needs above our ideals; this was a good decision. At this school they were with kids from many different ethnic backgrounds; they got a very international experience. The majority of the kids were MK's, a commonality existed among them that gave my children a sense of normalcy. The teachers and the principal themselves were missionaries, so they helped us to foster in our children an understanding of missions and a love for the nationals. This made for a very pleasant environment through which our kids could view missions and the country in which they were living. Some of the teachers and most of the staff members were Romanian, which gave the kids very positive exposure to the people we served. The children took language classes and learned to abandon the fear that this unknown country held for them.

Later, in the Czech Republic, we put our kids in a national school. Even our oldest, David, in sixth grade attended for a year. This was his own idea—something he wanted so he could learn some language and know the culture. This is one of many amazing decisions that my kids have made based on their own senses of identity as missionaries. I still believe national schools ultimately represent the best solution. Your kids need to identify with their adopted culture. If doing this through school is not an option, then find some activity for them in which they are involved with nationals. Avoid shielding your children from the difficulties that accompany cross-cultural living. Often in these difficulties they learn the most about God and His faithfulness. In David's case the year was very difficult, but even today he testifies that during that time he grew spiritually like never before, because every day just to survive He had to rely on God. Our daughter, Lauren, graduated from an elementary Czech school, went to a British private school, and now attends an MK school. Each situation had its unique challenges, but God always was ready to provide what was needed. However just as you don't want to avoid a situation just because it will be difficult, don't invite tough times for the sake of your ministry. In kindergarten our youngest child, Andrew, had trouble with stuttering. We explored alternative ways for him to learn in case the stuttering was caused by the stress of a dual-language situation. Ultimately do what is best all-around for your children. Your children are your ministry—given by God. Be good stewards of all that God has given you.

Becoming bilingual

Many people will tell you that when children move to the mission field, they will become fluent before you do. "Children learn so quickly," they say. Well, sometimes they do; sometimes they don't. Having unrealistic expectations can harm the child. Each child is different and will become bilingual at his or her own pace. Keep in mind these important things:

• Each child has his or her own learning style. We wondered why our oldest two children never learned the language very well at all. When we moved overseas, they were 2 and 4. We thought they would pick up the language quickly. But as they grew older, we found that our oldest is not the type of child to learn from his surroundings. He is a very concrete learner and doesn't trust his own senses enough to pick up behavior from those around him. He needs to know that something is right before he tries it. Being this way he was not the type of kid to go out on a playground and go home speaking the language. Had he been old enough to read, he could have learned it from lessons. But at this age he had only one way, and he didn't take to it. His little sister copied him in all that he did. From a young age she adopted his uneasiness and fears in this area. Thus neither learned the language until they became old enough to read and write it. Even then they were not conversational. Had we stayed longer, I think they would have been. By the end of our fifth year both had lost their fear and were willing to try without shame. (In fact, on moving to the Czech Republic our daughter, Lauren, attended Czech school and without any study became surprisingly fluent.) Our third child, Jessica, had no difficulties at all. From her babysitter and neighborhood children she picked up all she needed to know. She was more of a textbook case than were the other two. Andrew, our youngest, for three years has been in preschool a few hours a week. He has great understanding but still doesn't like to speak it much.

• If possible spend the majority of your fellowshiping time with nationals who do not speak English. One of the problems in many European countries is that EVERYBODY speaks English. Unless you are looking for an opportunity, for a long time you can avoid speaking the language. But your time of language acquisition needs to be concentrated even when it is difficult. Expecting your children to try to speak the language with people they barely know on the playground or at church is a mistake. When you are with people you know and like, everyone speaks English. Of course the very reason you know and like them is your common knowledge of English. We naturally are drawn to people with whom we can communicate. It's easier that way. But making friends with and spending time with those people who speak no English is wiser. If you get to know these people and your children can see that you like them and are trying to understand them, then they will be more likely to try to do the same.

Having a national childcare worker is a wonderful opportunity for the kids to learn the language. At first many parents are wary of having a babysitter who doesn't speak English. Leaving your children with someone who can't fully communicate with you is a frightening experience. However I think our babysitting situation was a major factor in the speed with which our children spoke the language. With David and Lauren their babysitter was a native Romanian, but she spoke English and couldn't bring herself to use Romanian with them. At the time we were somewhat relieved, but in looking back we see that we were wrong. This was the Romanian person that they trusted and loved most. At her house, in contrast to the playground, they felt safe.

At the beginning, had they taken for granted that they needed to try to understand her, they eventually would have. But they balked. Being the softhearted mother that she was, the babysitter broke under pressure from two adorable children. For a whole year they were in her care from four to five hours a day. They learned through this that they didn't HAVE to speak the language if they didn't want to. They didn't want to speak it. By the time Jessica was 2 (about three years later), we had a babysitter who spoke no English. We didn't think twice about this, because we could communicate just fine and knew that our child was in good hands. Jessica immediately started talking Romanian with her and her child and never thought anything of it.

While you are in language school, if you have young children, you will need child care. As tough as the first days will be, you are wise to insist that this person speak only the native language with your children. If they don't think that they have an easier way, they will learn out of necessity. Even though this national may do things a little differently than you do, if in front of your children you can communicate faith in this person, this will help your children immensely. This babysitter will be their first consistent contact with the new culture. If they see that you trust this person, then they will begin to trust her, too, and learn from her.

Being a normal parent

Being missionary parents really isn't that different from being parents in any other situation. Be tuned into your kids' needs and fears, watch them for signs of difficulty, keep the lines of communication open, and entrust them fully to God. Sometimes we tend to blame the mission field for a host of problems that would be present in any environment. Remember that the most important people in your child's life are you and the members of your immediate family. No matter where you live, you will be together as a unit. If your family is stable and solid, then kids can deal with most things they encounter. When you take them away to a new country, making sure that this family unit stays normal is important. Schedules, family devotions, rules, and routines are important factors in establishing normalcy in their lives. As weird as everything may seem, home is very much their world. You can make home anywhere.

QUESTIONS FOR DISCUSSION

1. Do you expect your host culture to challenge you in the area of parenting? In what ways?

2. What are some ideas of how to involve your kids in ministry?

3. Discuss giving your children to God—the difficulties and joys of it.

4. Make a list of the things you need to keep in check in your own life (be specific and personal) in order to teach your kids by example (i.e. tongue, jealousy, complaints, etc.). If you can, discuss these with the group.

5. Talk about some "routine" activities that can help you keep normalcy in your family.

6. Spend time in prayer committing your children to God. Ask Him to help you treasure them as well as to release them to Him.

Chapter 8

Left Behind

Just as we have children whom we dearly love and struggle to release to the Lord, so do our parents. Sending us across the ocean to do mission work sometimes is the most difficult thing they've ever done in their lives. Or maybe in your case parents aren't the ones who grieve most; it is adult children or an uncle or a sister. Whatever the case you most certainly have left someone behind. The departure has not been without grief, and, more often than not, without opposition.

Maybe they don't understand your call or your passion; maybe they don't understand how God is at work; or maybe they do understand but don't want to say goodbye anyway. Usually they are scared they may never see you again or they won't know your children or you won't know theirs, or that you won't need them anymore. Maybe they're afraid that they will need you and you won't be there. Sometimes they are a little fatalistic and assume that God is taking you away from them forever and that they must brace themselves for the worst. "Missions" to them means certain martyrdom. Whatever the cause of the reluctance, the majority of missionaries' families indeed are reluctant to say goodbye. This really is a very good thing. Some people are easier to love from a distance. If your loved ones actually looked forward to your leaving, you may have cause for worry.

Once my mom asked me how the parents of our colleagues dealt with their children's leaving. She had assumed that she was the only one who struggled and cried at the prospect of her youngest daughter flying so far away from the nest. She was surprised and probably a bit relieved to find out that she was very normal. The majority of us on the mission field have parents and relatives and friends who would give anything to have us home again. Certainly they support us, but they wish—oh, how they wish!—that we were called to be a little closer to home.

Understanding the emotions

The most important thing for you, as a missionary, is to understand and expect the emotions that these folks may have. This is tough to do if the strength of their opposition takes you by surprise. Remember that it probably took them by surprise, too. Many missionaries tell of how their moms and dads led the mission clubs at church and raised money to send others, yet when one of their children gave his or her life to missions, they recoiled at the thought. This doesn't make any sense, but it happens nonetheless. I've met other missionaries who have had to leave their grown children in order to follow the missions call. The children have voiced that they feel abandoned or unloved. How painful to say goodbye in the face of guilt and blame and hurt! At such a time you struggle to understand how perfect strangers that you have met with the mission organization can understand your heart better than can the ones who know you best. You may feel betrayed at worst or lonely at best and feel terribly misunderstood.

But as much as their behavior may hurt or shock or stun, the most important thing to remember in your response to them is never to put any amount of shame on the loved ones you leave behind. They are hurting in the midst of one of the biggest spiritual struggles of their lives. They don't need your criticism; they need your love and prayers. Because they love you so much, they struggle. Often they have heaped enough guilt on

themselves to last a lifetime. They often know that their attitudes are wrong but believe that they can't control the tidal
wave of grief and fear overtaking them.

The tough thing about this situation is that often these are
the very people that you count on to be the support for you.
Instead you find that you need to be the support for them. You
may feel angry that you have to play this role and may long for
them to respond to you with wisdom and strength. This is especially true in the case of leaving your mom and dad. You, too,
are struggling and don't have the energy to bear your own pain
and theirs. You want someone to whom you can turn. The one
that always has been there for you isn't. This makes the pain
greater. Be careful that you don't allow the necessity to get
away from the pain force you to push these loved ones away and
make a chasm between you. Sometimes your obedience to God
indeed will put you at odds or will wedge between you and
someone you love. But let God be the one to decide that; don't
let yourself be the cause of this happening. Your love can be
greater than is their pain and grief. Let your response to them be
ruled by that love.

As much as you may believe you need them, give them
room to grieve. God is sufficient to bear your burdens; He can
fill the emptiness that their lack of understanding creates. Since
He is sufficient to meet you in this need, you can free them up
to work through their emotions in their timing or hopefully in
God's timing.

Don't allow their emotions to control you. Understand that
they are normal emotions but often are exaggerated and ampli-
fied by Satan. He's waging war against you and isn't too proud
to use your family in the process. Understand what you are
fighting against. Go to war on your knees, not with your mouth.
Give your loved ones to the Lord and trust that He will work in
them to give them understanding. When God called you to mis-

sions, your entire world was affected. Just as your call to missions includes your children that you take with you, it also includes those you leave behind. God knew this would happen. He wants to use each situation for His own glory.

When I left for the mission field, my parents felt a jumble of emotions. They hated the idea of us being so far away; to think about it almost made them physically ill. But at the same time they could see how God's hand had been at work to bring us to this place. They wanted God's best for us. After many heated discussions, tears, hugs, and prayers, we left. Like any other missionary I struggled with culture shock. Regularly I wrote to my mom to tell her about all of our experiences. One day she telephoned me and said that God had spoken to her about something and she needed to take care of it right away. She felt as though some of my problems adjusting occurred because she had not released me to the Lord and given me her full blessing when we left. Starting at that very moment she wanted to free me up to be who and what God wanted me to be. From that moment on my mom has been a different person. She still struggles with the distance, but she has supported me emotionally and given me to God. God did this in her life and in mine. It has been such a blessing.

You're not the first

This problem of people having to say goodbye to people and places they love has been an issue ever since the beginning of time. In the Old Testament we see it in the lives of many of God's people. Abraham had to leave his home, his relatives, and his father's house when God called him to go to Canaan. Jochebed had to give Moses up while Moses was just a child. Ruth left her home and her parents to follow the God of her mother-in-law, Naomi. David and Jonathan wept over each other when David had to leave to avoid being killed by Saul. This problem still was around in the days that Jesus walked on the earth. Several times in the gospels Jesus speaks to His disciples on this very subject. The first recorded conversation about this was between Jesus and a follower on the road who claimed that he would follow Jesus wherever He went, but he first needed to bury his father. Jesus rebuked him by saying in Matthew 8:22, *"Follow me and allow the dead to bury their own dead."* Most commentaries agree that this man's father wasn't dead yet. Jesus wasn't being harsh in not allowing him to attend a funeral. Jesus could see the tangled devotions of the man's heart. He wanted to stay near home UNTIL his father died; then he would be able to follow Jesus without having to make a choice. Jesus clearly states that a choice must be made.

This choice is made even more clear in Matt. 10:37 when He says, *"He who loves father or mother more than me is not worthy of Me; and he who loves son or daughter more than Me is not worthy of Me."* God knows that we only can have one primary love in our lives; our lives will revolve around this love. It must be Him, or we cannot claim to be His followers. This doesn't mean that all believers are asked to leave family and loved ones behind, but be willing to if God says "go."

At a young age Jesus in His own life also demonstrates this truth. In Luke 2:49 He stays behind in the temple. When they find Him, His parents rebuke Him. He says to them, *"Why is it you were looking for me? Did you not know that I had to be in my Father's house?"* His response states clearly that His first loyalty is to His Heavenly Father. He is respectful but seems gently to rebuke them for not already realizing where He is and why He is there. Though worrying over your child seems like a natural parental response, Jesus seemed to want more out of them. They responded to the situation not with spiritual insight and maturity, but as parents. Though it is a natural response, it is not the response that pleases God. Because they were focused on Jesus, their son, and not on God the Father, they didn't see God's plan in their son's life that day. This is the point at which so many of our loved ones are. They are spiritually blinded by their love for us and can't see the plans that God has for us.

Again later on in His life He reaffirms the proper priorities. In Matthew 12:46-50 we see Jesus preaching and His mother and brothers visiting Him. Instead of stopping His activities and talking to them, He uses this opportunity to challenge His listeners' thinking about relationships. He says, *" 'Who is My mother and who are My brothers?' And stretching out His hand toward His disciples, He said, 'Behold, My mother and My brothers! For whoever does the will of My father who is in heaven, he is My brother and sister and mother'"*. Jesus' God-given mission on this earth to draw men to Himself was first before any family relationships.

These verses seem to indicate that Jesus didn't have much love or respect for His family, but if we look deeper, we know that this is not true. In Matthew 15:4 Jesus refers to God's command to honor our Father and our Mother. If Jesus emphasized both honoring our mother and father and loving them secondary to Jesus, then the two things cannot be contradictory. Often our understanding of the two things is contradictory, especially if our loved ones define *honor* as putting them above the call of God on our lives. This is a false definition of *honor* and should not be heeded. We also see an example of Jesus showing honor to His mother while he was dying. John 19:26-27 says, *When Jesus therefore saw his mother, and the disciple whom He loved standing nearby, He said to his Mother, "Woman, behold, your son!" Then he said to the disciple, "Behold, your mother"*. These are among His very last spoken words. In this we see that

Jesus is caring for His mother and honoring her, though He is leaving her physically.

When he took on human nature, Jesus modeled the kind of sacrifice I am describing. Two verses in the Bible give us a glimpse of what He gave up for our sakes. Second Corinthians 8:9 says, *For you know the grace of our Lord Jesus Christ, that though he was rich, yet for your sake he became poor, that you through his poverty might become rich.* And Philippians 2:6-7 says about Christ, although He existed in the form of God: . . . *(he) emptied Himself, taking the form of a bond-servant, and being made in the likeness of men.* He gave up so much more than we ever could.

Through these examples we learn many things about leaving home. We learn that leaving is not synonymous with abandonment when God's call is on our lives. Abandonment is forsaking or deserting something that is our responsibility. Jesus told the man on the road without hesitation to leave His family and follow Him. We can conclude from this that the man's father wasn't his responsibility anymore but was an excuse. We learn that leaving doesn't contradict honoring our parents, because Jesus emphasized the importance both of honoring and following, and He demonstrates the honoring of His own mother while He was on the cross. We learn that leaving doesn't negate loving, because Jesus loves perfectly, and yet it is He Who commands us to love Him before we do our families. Follow the call as our forefathers did—without excuses, without guilt, without hesitation. Leave the responses of those we love in God's hands.

A hundredfold?

In His Word God promises us that if we leave our loved ones for His sake, then He will bless us. Mark 10:29-30 says, *"Truly*

I say to you, there is no one who has left house or brothers or sisters or mother or father or children or farms, for my sake and for the gospel's sake, but that he will receive a hundred times as much now in the present age, . . . and in the age to come, eternal life." God has promised us that He not only will bless us in the life to come for our sacrifice but that He also will bless us right here on this earth. The amazing thing is that this really is true. We have seen this happen in our own lives. Of course I don't have a hundred mothers or sisters or farms, but I have often marveled at the level of intimacy and comfort I have with colleagues and fellow believers. God has given us friends to whom we relate on a very deep level. The quality of that friendship is a hundred times what many of our relationships in the past have been. The camaraderie among missionaries is unique in its richness and in its endurance. As He promises, He really will meet your need for companionship and love.

Enjoy these blessings! Don't reject them because of guilt feelings. I've known people who, out of a sense of loyalty to their families, refuse to connect with people God brings into their lives on the mission field. Some people close their hearts to others because they want God to fix the harmed relationships within their families their departure causes and restore and increase the intimacy that they desire. But when they do this, they cheat themselves out of great blessings indeed. God always will satisfy our needs if we are not stubborn about through whom He satisfies them. God knows what you need and knows through whom He can bless you.

What is a blessing to us, however, is sometimes a very difficult thing for our loved ones. They don't want to be replaced and have a difficult time rejoicing with you that your needs are met without them. Flaunting these special relationships in front of those who struggle with your absence is not wise. God's special friends are a great blessing indeed, but no one ever replaces those whom God originally gave you. They need to know this up front. If you constantly talk about your mission family or your second mom or your children's "aunts" and "uncles" or your national "daughter", then your relatives back home will begin to think that they are obsolete in your life. Though they may be unable to reach across the miles to undergird you, as you need, they desperately need to know that they are cherished by you and that by LEAVING them, you aren't leaving THEM. It makes saying goodbye a lot easier.

Before leaving for the mission field I wrote this poem to my parents to express to them that I knew and appreciated the depth of their love for me and to acknowledge that I couldn't be doing what I was doing if they hadn't done so much for me.

IN YOUR ARMS

*In your arms I learned that I should never fear the night
That God would never let me leave His precious caring
    sight; and
In your arms I learned that I should never fear the day
When other people laughed and misunderstood my ways.*

*In your arms I learned that I should never fear the past
But to cherish precious memories that would forever last;
    and
In your arms I learned that I should not fear what's ahead
But trust in God to lead each step along the way instead.*

*You see, it's in your precious arms that I have grown to
    know
Of all the things I should not fear that strengthen me to go;
    and*

In your arms I know that I will always find my rest
And one who will encourage me to be my very best.

So I thank you for your precious arms that show His love
*   to me*
For through these arms I know that I've been blessed
*   especially.*

My parents aren't perfect and didn't throw me a going-away party when I left them to move thousands of miles away. They have struggled and cried. I have, too. But every word of this poem is true. God chose them to be my parents. He has blessed me greatly through their love and prayers. He used the home they established to rear me to know Himself; He used their weaknesses to mold me and their strengths to shape me. When I was a baby, they held me in their arms and wanted only the best for me and tried to provide that. Don't forget or minimize these things when we think about the call God has put on our lives. They may not be thrilled with the way God answered the prayers and dreams for us, but they did love us enough to pray the prayers and dream the dreams. God will help them work through the difficulties, but they need this honoring and gratefulness from us always.

Keeping connected

Leaving your loved ones behind never is an easy task, but you can do some things to keep your hearts connected. Share with them your vision. If they are extremely supportive of you, then they will be your best prayer warriors. If they are not, then maybe God will use this vision to soften their hearts and draw them to the Savior. Encourage them to be part of your team. Let them know that their participation in this part of life is important to you and important to Kingdom work.

Keeping in touch also is important. With email, the Internet, and airplanes you never are too far away from family. A few generations ago when someone left for the mission field, it was forever. Now that simply is not the case. Travel is easy; communication is instant. Use the sources available to keep up with your loved ones. They need to know what you are doing and what your life is like. In no way can they can fathom your life in this new country. Sharing new experiences without them will make them feel detached from you. Your contexts forever will be different.

If you can share with them as you experience the changes, you will have an easier time reconnecting when you get back home to them. Also, the more detached they are from you, the less likely they are to work through the feelings your leaving causes.

The next generation

Even more difficult than the loss of children sometimes can be the loss of grandchildren. The idea of those precious babies growing up thousands of miles away from Grandma's hugs often is more than many grandparents and parents can bear. Many just assume that their grandchildren will not know them. However this doesn't have to be the case. With intentional effort at maintaining relationships your grandchildren can know and love their grandparents no matter how far away they are. In fact one family testified that their MK grandchildren are closer to them than are their Stateside grandchildren because of the intentionality with which the missionary family put family relationships at the top of the priority list!

Young children or babies will have few memories of anything more than a moment after it's happened. Fortunately with a little help, your loved ones can be a fixture around your house through many different avenues and can be reminded of all the people that are a part of their lives. So much depends on you and your attitude. If you love your extended family and talk about them a lot—interjecting memories, funny stories, and happy times—your kids will pick up on how special they are. If you aren't close to those relatives and don't really miss them, then your children probably won't either. Of course as your kids grow their memories improve. You don't have to try so diligently to make your loved ones present in your homes. By the time children reach older childhood, their own memories will replace yours. Their relatives will be present in their own hearts and minds.

Throughout the years we have discovered many practical ways to keep the memories alive. Some of these ways we have created; others we have gleaned from our colleagues:

a. Pictures

Pictures are a very important part of a missionary home. Keeping many pictures of grandparents and aunts and uncles and cousins within sight is a constant reminder to your kids of who they are and to whom they are connected. When my kids were very young, we kept photo albums of times we had been with family. These albums had many pictures of the kids with their relatives. Each child had his or her own album. They loved looking through the pictures of themselves.

Seeing themselves in the midst of good times with relatives kept the memories alive. Sending pictures equally is important. It helps those back home to keep up with the changing faces of childhood. Kids change so quickly. If Grandmamma isn't kept updated on their latest looks, the feeling of estrangement when they meet again is overwhelming.

b. Telephone calls

Even when our children were very young, we would spend the money to allow them to talk to their relatives. They loved talking on the phone. The voice recognition was an important part of them "knowing" their loved ones.

c. Birthday parties

Birthdays are an important part of a child's life. Sharing these times with distant relatives helps them to connect. On the big day we would make sure that they had a gift from grandparents as well as receiving a telephone call to wish them happy birthday. Taking pictures of these events and sending them to your loved ones will help them celebrate with you. One idea that I thought was wonderful was having a birthday party for Grandmamma or Granddaddy on the grandparent's special day, even though they weren't with us. The family can wrap presents to send, have a cake, and take pictures to send with the presents.

d. Holidays

In the life of a child holidays are important. Special boxes from America are a wonderful surprise and something the kids joyously will anticipate. A box from Grandmamma always thrills our kids, even the teen-agers! Of course, with mail being what it is, we often had Christmas in phases, but whenever the packages arrived—sometimes early, often by Christmas, but just as often, in January—we made the best of it and just kept celebrating! Also sending presents home to Grandma is important. Let the kids be a part of choosing a gift or making a card.

d. Videos

Sending and receiving videos will do a lot to remind children who their loved ones are. We would send silly videos; the kids loved making them. Watching videos also was good because it reminded the kids what their relatives looked like and sounded like.

e. Email

As the kids get older, email is a wonderful means for staying in touch. My kids know more about the computer than I do. With instant messaging as easy as it is, they have set up accounts for their aunts and grandmothers. We have bought a web camera. Through the computer we now can type to each other, see each other, and even talk for free.

f. Regular updates

One good practice is to get the kids to sit down once a week to jot a quick note about an experience that week. They can compare your week with theirs. Adding humor helps! Often they picture you enduring hardship. When you can laugh about the difficulties, it encourages them.

g. Visits

Of course visits are wonderful. If your budget allows, do whatever is necessary to see each other on a regular basis. If you can't afford vacation time in the States, sometimes a church will pay for you to travel home. Make your needs known; trust God to meet them. I have been amazed at how the Lord three times has provided for us to go back to America besides our regular Stateside assignments. In His timing God will provide opportunities.

h. Stories

Another way our children have stayed connected is through stories. We tell them stories about our own childhoods, about what our parents or sisters did for, with, and sometimes to us. Then when we all get together, they say, "You mean SHE used to . . .?", or, "She's the one that made that bean bag you still have . . ..". "This is the one you used to ride horses with . . .."

Conclusion

Connecting to family is important to everyone involved. By moving overseas you are sacrificing a geographically close relationship with your relatives. You have no easy way around that. Your relationships will be different because of the call on your lives. But it doesn't have to be estranged, difficult, or even lacking. If you all work together with intentionality, it can be wonderful, encouraging, and fulfilling. Sometimes your relatives' not reciprocating can bring an added challenge. If this is the case, this may occur because they feel overwhelmed by the distance or don't understand how closeness can be maintained, so they don't try. In these cases, you'll have to carry the load. For your children's sakes and for your own, making the effort is worthwhile if for no other reason than for the rippling effect your ministry and calling will have on their lives.

Do you realize that YOU may be the pipeline through which your family members themselves become involved in missions? God has not called you in a vacuum. He will affect every person in your life through His calling of you. Let Him do His work through you. Don't wait for them to write you or travel to see you. Take it on yourself to make sure these things happen—for both your sakes and for the Kingdom.

QUESTIONS FOR DISCUSSION

1. How have your loved ones reacted to your leaving?

2. Put yourself in their shoes. How do you think you would react?

3. What are some ways you can communicate love to them through this difficult time?

4. Think about what practical things might help you cope with their absence (time with spouse, good friends, etc.) Ask God for these things.

5. How does Jesus' example help you in coping with this loss?

6. Write a poem or a letter to one person that you miss the most. Tell the person how you feel and how you are entrusting him or her to the Lord.

Chapter 9

All in the Family

When you enter the ranks of missionaries, you are born into a brand-new family. With this family you will laugh, cry, celebrate, and mourn. You'll never find other people who understand you quite as well as these guys do. With them you'll share a cross-cultural camaraderie that will set you apart from the rest of the world.

Only other missionaries fully can understand the changes that have taken place in you, the embarrassment of language blunders, the thrill of a successful shopping venture, and the warped sense of humor you develop through it all. With these people you will celebrate birthdays, mourn the loss of loved ones, and rejoice together at finding anything remotely resembling a Christmas turkey at Christmas.

As with all families, during your life together you will experience a whole range of circumstances. You'll have great fellowship and lifelong relationships, but you'll also have black sheep who go astray, authority figures you resent, treatment you believe you don't deserve, expectations both met and unmet, and many other variations of our corporate-sin natures revealed.

Living together in peace and harmony sometimes can seem impossible. Missionaries often say that their greatest challenge on the field is living peaceably with their colleagues. This is sad but true, so this is a heads-up for some of the situations that may loom in your future.

The head of the family: relating to authority

In this new family authority figures make the decisions; everybody else submits to them. Whether it's the governing board, top leader of the entire organization, or just the person directly over you, your spirit of cooperation and respect will be vital. As believers we may think that having a good attitude toward authority is a given, but often quite the opposite is true. In fact a distinct irony exists in mission structure, because the kind of people that become missionaries are ones that are highly motivated, driven, committed, and sure of their call. They are people of action with strong personalities and strong wills. Put all that personality and strong will in one room, and sparks can fly—that's a lot of "will per square inch"! Missionaries have a tough time surviving under leadership with which they don't agree. And no matter how qualified the authority figure might be, the other missionaries certainly won't agree with that person all the time. So, the dilemma exists.

Of course the typical missionary will spiritualize the conflict. He or she will claim to be willing to submit to God but not to poor leadership. The typical thinking goes, "The authority figure obviously isn't listening to God, because he is making decisions that I think are stupid, wasteful, hurtful, damaging, etc." This type of thinking results in gossip, slander, rebellious spirits, and discontentment. It also will damage relationships, the Lord's reputation, and the fruitfulness of your ministry.

During the past decade, if I've learned to lean on one phrase, it is "God is bigger than . . .." He's bigger than any organization, any supervisor, any problem, any dishonesty, any bad strategies, any restrictions, and any rules. He's also bigger than any personal issues we may have. He is bigger than anything that we see as an adversary. He ultimately is the one who has allowed you to be in the position you are in; He has put the authority figures over you; He has allowed the rules and restrictions to be in place over you; He has allowed it all. God is sovereign!

If you are upset about the way things are going, ultimately you need to take the matter up with God. In Isaiah 45:7 He says, *"[I am] The One forming light and creating darkness, causing well-being and creating calamity; I am the Lord who does all these."* If you are discontent, you are discontent with Him. If you are grumbling, you are grumbling against Him. If you are slandering, you are slandering Him. If you won't submit, He is the one to whom you are refusing your submission. He is the author of your circumstances. He is using these circumstances to make you more like Jesus.

What right do we have to resist His transforming touch in our lives? To do so will bring sorrow. *Woe to the one who quarrels with his Maker—an earthenware vessel among the vessels of earth! Will the clay say to the potter, "What are you doing?"* (Isa. 45:9).

To embrace our circumstances—to see them with spiritual eyes and allow them to transform us—will bring true joy and contentment. *For I have learned to be content in whatever circumstances I am,* said Paul. *I know how to get along with humble means, and I also know how to live in prosperity; in any and every circumstance I have learned the secret of being filled and going hungry, both of having abundance and suffering need. I can do all things through Him who strengthens me* (Phil. 4:11-13).

When we are God's children, we never are the victims. He will strengthen us. He will defend and protect us. *The Lord will protect you from all evil; He will keep your soul* (Ps. 121:7). How can we be victimized when we are under His protection? This is impossible. So we can embrace every situation as if it is from Him, because He has the power to change it. If you know anything of God's character, you know that He is good. His intention in allowing you to be in your situation is for good. He is making you more like Christ, just as He promised. He will teach you, use you, mold you, and change you through your circumstance.

I love Romans 8:28, but often it is misunderstood. It doesn't say that everything we experience is good. Anyone who has ever tried to learn a foreign language knows this! What it says is that for those of us who love Jesus and are walking in His will through the power of His Spirit, for us He will bring about good out of anything that happens to us. Just look at Joseph! No one could possibly think that being thrown in a pit, betrayed by his brothers, and sold into slavery was a good thing. It was horrific. But God turned it into something good for Joseph, because Joseph loved God and was living according to God's purpose for Him. Joseph himself said to his brothers, *"You meant evil against me, but God meant it for good . . ."* (Gen. 50:20). He will do the same for you.

Instead of complaining pray that God will give you the grace to withstand your circumstances. He can turn the hearts of kings like channels of water. He certainly can take care of one little missionary who has authority over you or one little circumstance that is impeding your ministry—if indeed that missionary or that circumstance is the problem. But here is a warning—more often than not, prayer will result in YOUR heart being changed!

Sometimes your problem isn't a leader with whom you don't agree; it's a leader you don't know. In our fluid missionary environment new leadership is not unusual. When leadership changes, goals, strategies, and visions also change. You are expected to get behind these new ideas and methods and support the new plan. Sometimes switching gears is difficult; more often than not, we just plain don't want to do this. Unless we are careful, repeated change can cause us to become cynical.

During these times remember who the real boss is. You are where you are because God called you there. His goals and visions for you never have changed. If the new leader or the new strategy is something you cannot in good conscience follow, then you are better off leaving than staying and grumbling. But be careful of the hill on which you choose to die. Not many things would justify your surrendering your call. In fact your call will help you live with many things with which you disagree. Returning home simply because you can't get along with your supervisor will not give you a good reputation, nor will it benefit the cause of Christ. Without a strong conviction and a direct leading from the Lord, stay and trust that God will continue to use you under the new leadership.

Praying for your new leader also will be vital. He will need your intercession as He seeks God's will for the team. Have you ever noticed that having bad feelings toward someone for whom you are praying is very difficult? God has a way of giving us insight to the way that person is thinking and helps us to empathize with the person. As we begin to understand his motivations in light of this new insight, we pray effectively and feel less defensive. Believe it or not two sides always exist to every issue; both usually are legitimate. Praying allows God to put spiritual glasses on you and to see the other side. More often than not, when you are dealing with another missionary, the other person likely is trying to listen and obey God just as you are. Prayer will allow you to have a softer heart and will make having a critical spirit more difficult.

Submission is a spiritual exercise. Ephesians 5:18-21 commands us to be filled with the Holy Spirit and then offers some insight into what a Spirit-filled person is like: . . . *speaking* . . . *singing and making melody . . . giving thanks* . . . and lastly, ... being subject to one another . . .. Though that last sentence is separated in our Bibles, in the original language this part is grammatically identical to the other characteristics of being filled with the Spirit. Paul goes on to give some examples of Spirit-filled submission. He clarifies that the one to whom submission is given has a responsibility as well; it is not a passive activity. His examples include wives to husbands, husbands to wives, children to parents, and slaves to masters. This last example easily can be applied to working relationships (no sarcasm here, please!).

Transition in the family: the revolving door of missionary relationships

Missionary life really can affect your heart. From moments of absolute delight to crushing heartache, you'll feel every emotion. One of the most common among the "family" is a sense of loss because their "relatives" keep moving away. Missionaries are so transient, especially in today's world of new directions, new ideas, and new approaches. With the urgency of the task, the mobility made possible through air travel, and the wealth of knowledge that we possess about people groups because of the computer age, the missionary who serves 25 years in the same place and retires from that position seems to be getting more and more rare. Serving a lifetime easily can be a tour of three or more countries, people groups, or even continents. This mobility often leads to a sense of detachment from any meaningful relationships. We have had to say goodbye to our family, friends, and colleagues so many times that doing so becomes blasé. The first few times our best friends from the field move away, our hearts break. They have become our family—our security. But after this happens over and over again, we tend to harden our hearts to keep them from breaking. Goodbyes occur easily, we don't stop to shed a tear; we try not to think about it anymore. But this response is very unhealthy and also robs us of all that God wants to give us through this relationship—whatever length of time it lasts.

Often new people arrive on the field and don't understand the walls that older missionaries have built around their hearts to protect them from the pain of loss. I was like that. After being on the field a few years I understood the protective layer that I had seen early on but figured a better way had to exist.

And then our turn occurred. God called us somewhere else. We had to be the ones to break hearts. I then determined that I didn't have to say goodbye completely. God had given us precious relationships; they were important enough to preserve. I decided to invest in keeping the precious gift God had given me. I still make a point to call, write, and keep in touch with and pray for each of the special friends that through the years God has given me. I have learned from them and taken something away that enriched my life. If I continue my efforts, I will have friends worldwide! I will be richer for my experiences and not be heartbroken. But making the effort is necessary.

This effort is not just for our sakes but is for the sakes of others as well. With short-termers arriving and going and colleagues leaving the field for various reasons, a person easily can demonstrate an attitude of "out of sight, out of mind." However this attitude will leave your colleagues feeling cut off, hurt, and lonely. Whether the people were on the field six months or 20 years, you became important to them. They became somewhat distant to their own families. As they readjust to life in the U.S., helping them know that the bonds formed while overseas were real and meaningful is important. Make a point to contact these former colleagues and to keep them connected to their former team. Remaining a true and lasting friend is vital if the body of Christ is to exist in a healthy manner. The people with whom He has given you to work are people He intentionally planned for you to know. Don't discard them without a thought. Of course we don't have time to keep in touch with every person we've ever worked alongside, but as God gives relationships to you, treasure them and don't toss them aside casually when distance and life changes keep you apart.

Family matters: responding to difficulties within the missionary family

Working with other missionaries is both a joy and a challenge as we seek to glorify God together. When conflict erupts between two or more members, the whole body suffers.

a. Public disputes
One of the biggest challenges occurs when we see our colleagues in some sort of public dispute with the organization or with another colleague. Though we may not want to take sides, we cannot remain untouched by the conflict. Conflict always has a ripple effect and will cause some waves in your life. So what are you to do?

Keep the peace at all cost, choose a side and take a stand, or stand to the side and watch it play out? Each situation is different, but here are some basic guidelines for dealing with a conflict.

• Always stand for truth. It must not be compromised. If you are drawn into the conflict, don't let loyalty to a friend or loyalty to your organization take the place of truth. Speak the truth in love and without regret.

• Prayer is a key to dissolving any conflict. Intercede for the parties involved. God very well may give you enough insight into the situation that you can help resolve the conflict.

• Keep your mouth shut! Gossip and slander will do no one any good. If you have something to say, say it to the person it concerns. If you can't do that, don't say it at all.

• Trust in God's sovereignty and continue to act in love toward both parties. Both members of the conflict probably are trying to act on their convictions and beliefs. Though you might disagree with one or the other or maybe both, you don't have to lose faith in them completely. Just as God works in you, He is working in them. He promises to complete His work. You can trust Him in that. If one of the members is working outside of God's will, He has the power and ability to make that known to the person, to teach the person, and to restore him or her.

• Be prepared for God to use you in this restorative process. This will require your becoming familiar with basic principles of confrontation as well as with biblical procedures for arguments and disputes. In Matthew 18 and Galatians 6:1 you can find these procedures.

b. Sinful behavior

Even more devastating is to find that one of your colleagues has had to leave the field because of divorce, immorality, or some type of ethical issue. This is both heartbreaking and eye-opening. We easily can believe that we are beyond the reach of such issues, but that misunderstanding very well may leave you open and vulnerable to such attacks by Satan. Many missionaries find that once they get away from their normal parameters, sin crops up in unexpected places. Some are shocked to find themselves struggling with pornography, marital difficulties, dishonesty, and sexual sin. Be aware of the depravity of your own heart and the lengths to which Satan will go to destroy you. Be on your guard and be in prayer for your colleagues. *Let him who thinks he stands take heed, lest he fall* (1 Cor. 10:12).

c. Sent packing

One of the biggest surprises in my first few years on the field was when a fellow missionary was sent home—fired, if you will. I never thought about a missionary being fired. How can you fire someone who wants to work for God? This seemed so cruel and hurtful. But it does happen. In our case a worker was sent to fill a position for which she was totally unqualified. Her interests were not in keeping with the position at all; it caused much grief and conflict on the team. She was asked to leave. I assumed she would be devastated. She may have been, but she went back to the States and got another assignment which matched her perfectly. For years we kept up with her. In her new place of service she was a real gift—highly praised and lauded as an answer to prayer.

I was glad that God took care of this co-worker and used her. But the reality that being "fired" was a possibility on the mission field opened my eyes to the fact that just because we're doing God's work doesn't mean that we're not accountable to do it well. Doing your work "as unto the Lord" doesn't mean slacking but quite the opposite.

The extended family: relating well with churches back home

Churches and supporters back home also are an important part of the family. You represent their link to the mission field. See them as your partners in ministry. As such, keep them abreast about what is happening in your part of the world. As busy as you are and as tough as doing so is, stay in touch! These are your prayer partners and need to know how to pray. A key to a good relationship with home churches and supporters is communication. Common problems with communication are knowing when to talk and when to listen.

Churches need to know what you need from them. Often they want to be a part of what you're doing but have no idea how to do it. Tell them about your work and how they can pray for you. Share with them about your life, your struggles, and your needs. In a good relationship being honest is important. Especially as you prepare to go home on furlough or Stateside assignment, those supporting people and churches want to help meet your needs. Let them! Make your needs known! (A note of caution: your organization, like mine, may have policies and guidelines regarding what kinds of needs—particularly financial—to make known to constituents and how the missionary is to deal with this. Definitely observe those.)

On the flip side is the problem of the missionary's expecting too much from home churches or supporters and having an attitude of entitlement. If you expect that churches are just there to support and pamper you and if you have no sense of responsibility toward them, you will err by appearing discourteous, rude, and thoughtless. As you plan for your time in the States, remember that if you plan to stay in a missionary residence or use a borrowed vehicle, these things need to be appreciated, not expected. Don't abuse the special role God has given you!

Communication is a real key. Communicate well in advance; let the church know of any change in plans. Some home churches complain that missionaries reserve their houses and then, without any notice, change their plans. This will cause hard feelings and much inconvenience, since the church may have turned others aside for you. All churches have expectations for missionaries staying in their homes. They also have policies in place for the missionary house. These may include such matters as payment of bills or upkeep. Be sure these are clearly stated and understood. Failure to do this will result in strained relationships and sometimes embarrassment. On our first Stateside, when my husband went to pay the utility bill, the church secretary said, "Don't worry about it." He thought she meant that the church would take care of the utility bill. Whatever she said and whatever Preston understood, that's not what the church was thinking. Church members thought we had left them with a family-size utility bill. They even revised their house policy and now require a utility deposit and a written agreement. We felt terrible for the misunderstanding, but we learned a valuable lesson.

Another shocking thing that happened on Stateside was learning how differently churches around the U.S. view missionaries. We split our Stateside assignment time between our two families. In one area we genuinely were surprised by the generosity of churches. Every time we did anything, we seemed to be given some gift. One can get accustomed to that very easily! Then in another area the normal gift was a pat on the back. At one missions conference where Preston participated, all the missionaries received a very generous honorarium; at another, two months later, less than 300 miles away, nothing. Nothing in the world was wrong with either situation. But after getting used to the generosity of our first home, we had developed expectations. The point is this: make sure your expectations don't take the joy out of sharing with any church that wants to hear.

Conclusion

Missionaries are great folks. You'll love being a part of this large, loving, exciting family. But sometimes, just as in the movie *My Big Fat Greek Wedding*, they will drive you crazy. Treasure these folks that God has put in place around you to teach you, love you, challenge you, and encourage you. But understand that they need for you to live with them with a lot of gra.e, mercy, and understanding. We are to love our brothers and sisters in Christ. The 1 Corinthians-type of love isn't for wimps. I challenge you to exercise this type of love with your new family.

QUESTIONS FOR DISCUSSION

1. Are you struggling to relate rightly to someone on the field—a supervisor, colleague, or someone else? Spend time praying for this person specifically and commit to continue praying daily for the person.

2. Make a list of people that you have known on the mission field that now are gone. Do any believe that you have abandoned them because of their departure? If so commit to contact them through email, letter, or phone call.

3. Are you in regular contact with friends and supporting churches? Discuss with your group how you might make a plan to have contact with those people and churches that God has brought into your life. Adopt ideas from your colleagues and share your own.

4. Discuss what some practical ways are to make your needs known without violating policy or cultivating a feeling of entitlement.

5. Read 1 Corinthians 13. Examine your own attitude toward you new family and evaluate how you measure up to this standard. Pray with one person in your group about this.

Conclusion

Moving to a new culture often will leave you with the feeling that nothing is quite real. Their standards aren't your standards; their social expectations aren't yours to worry about, their money looks and feels like monopoly money, and giving it away without a thought is only too easy. In a way it all seems surreal at first. Because we lived the closest to the airport in Bucharest, we often were called on to pick up new colleagues arriving on the field. I never ceased to get tickled when they began to give away their money to the guys helping with the luggage. They would just fan out this wad of money and say, "Here you go; how much you want?" No, not really, but the situation seemed about that bad. To them this was like living in a pretend world. Nothing had taken on that feel of reality yet. For so many of us, until that long trip across the ocean, we were somewhat unaware that other cultures that existed and survived without our rules and expectations

In some ways this new reality is unnerving, because you are viewed differently and often misunderstood. But in another way one can feel very free to be not above but apart from the expectations of your countrymembers. In this new culture living up to what society says is right is not your goal, because so often what society says is right simply eludes you. For a blessed short time before you learn the language and the culture, you are free to act and think on your own without the strain of worrying about what someone else will think.

This is the perfect time to concentrate on becoming an aroma of Christ. As you don't know how to correctly respond to situations, let your responses be measured and determined by the culture of Christ. As you feel lonely and isolated, spend extra time in God's Word to build up your spiritual strength for the challenges that lie ahead. As you question your ministry possibilities, let them be shaped and honed not by need but by commission. In a big way this is a chance to begin at ground zero. You have no reputation and no cultural hangups—you are a free agent. Use this for your benefit.

This period also will be a time to re-think many of the assumptions you have held since you were old enough to have assumptions. Allow God to reshape your worldview, your reality, your understanding. Often whenever we are in a new situation, we try to make all of the unknowns fit into our known parameters. We are better off if we allow God to change our parameters. During this time the opportunities to learn and grow in Christ are phenomenal.

One example of this in my life was realizing that "living up to the Joneses" was a reality in Romania just as it was in America. That seemed amazing to me as I looked at what these people had and what they wanted. The desired end was so far below our standard of living, I just couldn't believe anyone would long for it. I thought people were ridiculous for coveting another's home when the homes they were coveting were worse than were the housing projects in the towns in which I had lived. To me the situation was laughable. I wanted to shake them and say, "Hey, can't you see this is not worth getting jealous over?"

But instead of God leaving me in this state of superiority, He used this opportunity to teach me a new truth. He showed me that my covetousness was just as ridiculous to Him, the King of Heaven, as theirs was to me. All the riches of the richest in America are nothing compared with what He has for us in heaven, yet our hearts long for these temporal riches instead. How ridiculous that must be to God! I wanted to help Romanians realize my reality as their own, but God had other plans. He used the new set of circumstances to help me re-evaluate my own values in light of His eternal perspective.

Another area in which we needed a reality check was in the area of finances. Leaving your country a poor missionary in need of other people's financial assistance (at least in their opinion) and arriving in your new home country, only to realize that you are rich, is the strangest thing! Of course if you are a missionary in Vienna or the Swiss Alps, this may not be the case, but in most cases, the country in which you find yourself is not nearly as wealthy as America is. Thus, even on your frugal budget, you are much better off financially than those you are there to serve. This was a shock to me. In Romania poverty was measured on a whole different scale. For middle-class America not having money means having only one car in the family, shopping at garage sales, and buying used furniture. It does not mean that you eat meat only on holidays, do your laundry by hand, and wear the same clothes for a week. My stories of woe about how we had had no money while we prepared to go the mission field were a mockery to people who have no front teeth because they couldn't afford toothpaste or dental care.

Our first tendency when we arrived in this new world was to deny the fact that we were rich. We certainly never had felt rich before, so our instinct was to explain how misguided the nationals were and explain that we really were poor; they just didn't know it. But the more we gave that story, the less credible it sounded even to us. God began to show us that not only in the eyes of these people, but in reality, we have been given so much and indeed are rich.

Through situations like these we were able to re-evaluate the way we looked at our own lives and the way we judged our circumstances. Because for a time we felt like people without a country and without a society to guide us, we had to find a new plumbline. This took us to our knees and forced us to depend on God in a way we hadn't done previously. This dependence on God is where the aroma of the knowledge of Him begins. As we sit at His feet and learn of Him, we absorb His fragrance. Paul says *"it is no longer I who live, but Christ lives in me" (Gal 2:20).* When we are full of Him, then we smell of Him; then God is able to spread through us the fragrance of Him in every place. In our marriage, with our children, in our ministry, in our quiet times, with our families back home, in the midst of disappointments, in the times of greatest joy. God wants us to be full of Him so that He can work through us. This is the ultimate goal of any missionary—to be the conduit through which God freely works.

I encourage you as you embark on this—the greatest journey of obedience and faith—to sit at Jesus' feet. Don't go to do a task or to accomplish a goal or to make a difference. Go to serve Jesus. Although learning the culture of the people that you serve is important, it cannot be your only goal. Although winning these people to Christ is of utmost importance, this can't be your goal either. Paul was a wonderful example of what the goal of a missionary should be. His example is the only way to be successful. Listen to what he says in 1 Corinthians 2:1-5 (NIV): *When I came to you, brothers, I did not come with eloquence or superior wisdom as I proclaimed to you the testimony about God. For I resolved to know nothing while I was with you except Jesus Christ and Him crucified. I came to you in weakness and fear, and with much trembling. My message and my preaching were not with the wise and persuasive words, but with a demonstration of the Spirit's power, so that your faith might not rest on men's wisdom, but on God's power.*

Does this sound like the heartcry of most missionaries or Christian workers you know? Don't we too often have an attitude of superiority or giftedness? I rarely have heard one speak as humbly as Paul. The trick is not in being rich in talents but rich in Christ. Paul talks about being an aroma. He demonstrates not his intelligence and his understanding of their culture but the Spirit's power. You can study preaching and discipleship for years, but until you absorb the very fragrance of the knowledge of Christ, your preaching will be powerless and your discipleship uninspired—empty. This knowledge, this absorption of His aroma occurs only through time on your knees and in the Word. The focus of what Paul says is God, not himself—Christ and nothing else. This can be our heart. Everything is about Him.

Sometimes when we speak of being an aroma of Christ, the impossibility of the task before us can be overwhelming. But God is aware of what He is dealing with. Further down from the verse about being an aroma in 2 Corinthians is another verse that puts this in perspective. Second Corinthians 4:7-9 says, *But we have this treasure in jars of clay to show that this all-surpassing power is from God and not from us. We are hard pressed on every side, but not crushed; perplexed but not in despair; persecuted, but not abandoned; struck down, but not destroyed.*

With our horrible tendency to think that we, ourselves, are something great, God found keeping us trapped in these jars of clay to be necessary. He has given us a great ability—to absorb Christ—to be fragrant. But if left to ourselves, we would pat ourselves on the back for smelling so good and forget from whom we got the smell. God safeguards us against this pride by allowing our sinful flesh to remain a part of us until Christ returns. Until that day we will feel the tension of living in two worlds, but this pressure will not destroy what God has begun in us. You will have difficult times and will see the ugliness of your own heart, but you never will disappoint God. He knows of what you are made and He knows the work that He has begun in your heart. Mostly He knows which of these is going to have the final victory. Don't make it your goal to be an aroma, or your sinful heart will turn your eyes from Jesus and make your efforts self-centered. Instead make your goal to know Jesus. Then, without even trying, you will be an aroma.

Hannibal Books

is an Evangelical Christian book-publishing company

To order more copies of
Being an Aroma of Christ
at $12.95 each plus shipping

Call us toll free:

1-800-747-0738

Write us:

P.O. Box 461592
Garland, TX 75046

Visit our web site:

www.hannibalbooks.com

FAX us toll free:

1-888-252-3022

Email us:

orders@hannibalbooks.com

Order directly from Hannibal Books

Be a 24/7 Christian by Wade Akins. Want to make Jesus truly the Lord your life but don't know how? This renowned missionary evangelist/strategist tells how to live the adventure of being totally sold out to the Lord every moment of every day, every day of every year.

_____Copies at $9.95=_____

Rescue by Jean Phillips. Missionaries Jean Phillips and husband Gene lived through some of the most harrowing moments in African history of the last half century. Abducted and threatened with death, Jean and Gene draw on God's lessons of a lifetime.

_____Copies at $12.95=_____

Beyond Surrender by Barbara J. Singerman. A dramatic story of one family's quest to bring light to a dark and desperate world. The Singerman family serves in Benin, West Africa. They confront spiritual warfare beyond anything they expect when they surrender to missions.

_____Copies at $12.95=_____

The Man in the Green Jeep, by Viola Palmer. Enjoy this captivating glance into children's lives and culture in Central America; see missionaries at work.

____Copies at $9.95 = _____

Add $3.00 postage and handling for first book, 50 cents for each additional book.

Shipping & Handling: _____

TX residents add 8.25% sales tax: _____

**Total Enclosed
(check or money order)** _____

Name _____

Address_____

City_____State_____Zip_____

Phone _____ Email _____

See address and other contact information on page 143